TRAIL OF FEARS

ELLIE CHAMBERLAIN

Published in paperback in 2016 by Sixth Element Publishing
on behalf of Ellie Chamberlain

Sixth Element Publishing
Arthur Robinson House
13-14 The Green
Billingham TS23 1EU
Tel: 01642 360253
www.6epublishing.net

ISBN 978-1-908299-97-0

British Library Cataloguing in Publication Data. A catalogue record for this book is
available from the British Library.

Printed in Great Britain.

To Isaac:

thank you for walking through
the landscape of colour with me.

I told them that they should never deny a writer her voice.
I whispered, but they ignored me.
I spoke, but they refused to listen.
I shouted louder, but they turned their backs.

This is the result.
This is my voice.

I am an artist but I do not understand colour. I cannot feel it, breathe it, love it or live it. My life is a black and white collision of colourless grey. Grey days. Grey thoughts. Grey nights. As I child, I ran in the colourless rainbows but the cloud of fear was never far away:

I was born in fear.
I lived and grew up in fear.
I was brainwashed by fear.
What would happen if
one day I faced the fear?

CHAPTER 1

The voices in my head were of 'those people'. In a desperate need to escape and breathe in some fresh air, I grab my coat and make a dive for the door before I talk myself out of it. 'But what if you see one of 'those people'?' My internal voices are concerned for my safety and sanity. 'What if you bump into one of them and have to have one of those awkward conversations?'

'How are you?' They will innocently ask.

'Oh, I am fine.' I will lie.

'We miss you.' A dramatic pause ensues in anticipation of an outpouring of emotion.

'I know. I won't be back.' Try to show no emotion.

'We know. But we miss you and love you.' Look of pity. Awkward silence.

I have played out this scenario too many times both in reality and in my head. The only other alternative to these impromptu awkward discussions is the one where thirty years of friendship disappears in a tortured look of 'let's pretend we haven't seen each other', or a brief 'hello' and failure to stop. Either way, I hate the visible invisibility that seems to cloak me to 'those people.'

It is a cold October day but the sun has just fought through the earlier rain clouds and the rusty leaves are crying pellets of ammunition on my shoulders as

I walk towards the river. I am hoping the murky waters will provide inspiration to help me make my decision, although deep down I know it has already been made, I just need the confidence to follow it through. Stopping at the bridge, I lean over the rusty railing to take in a rare moment of solitude as the river sings a tune that only I can hear. The leaves and twigs dance to the rhythm of the day and it is wonderfully mesmerising. In that moment, I realise that no matter what obstacles are placed in your way in life they float downstream, like broken twigs. If you are willing to surrender to an inevitable lack of control they will eventually float by, but in the same way that the river remains constantly flowing with the breeze, so can you. Sometimes it overflows with emotion, sometimes it shrinks silently back into the banks, but it is constant in the way it keeps moving and adjusting to the conditions imposed upon it by the elements. We can learn a lot from watching a river.

I am still hurting. You go through stages people told me, anger, grief, loss, the list seems endless, but they are right. The problem is that each day is different and the myriad of emotions is never-ending. I feel as though my life has turned upside down and suddenly I am walking in the sky and banging my head on the ground.

Turning around, I walk hand in hand with the river allowing the frozen air to excite my lungs, I feel it cleansing my pain. Can the river's energy baptise me with renewed vision and strength? I hadn't realised before how far I had been manipulated into losing my confidence and self worth but now it is becoming screamingly obvious. I simply don't know how to escape and find the person I was before, unless I take this one chance and face my demons head on. I reach the end of the river's path and the sudden meeting with civilisation jolts me back into the present. A main road thrusts itself in my face, shouting with busy pedestrians locked in their own problems and impatient motorists concentrating only on their own unfulfilled journey. I decide to cross the road, I don't really know why, but at this stage I am just going where the road takes me. Stopping at the kerb, my eyes fixate on the traffic lights of the pedestrian crossing as I wait anxiously for the green man to appear. The panic at being surrounded by people begins to creep in and simultaneously I feel vulnerable. Suddenly, I become distracted by a small elderly gentleman crossing alongside me and my panic rises as I worry that he won't be able to cross this busy road in time. I know how he feels, I am anxious myself, but I needn't have worried, as with a brisk flick of his stick he navigates safely across just before the lights change and the traffic roars ahead, beating me to the edge of the kerb.

'They don't give you much time to cross, do they?' I comment in a feeble attempt to explain why I am staring at the poor chap until he is safe. His reply is not what I expect.

'I like it when you have a long wait for the lights to change, it makes you live longer. If you are waiting longer, you have a longer life, no?' His eyes twinkle like a cheeky schoolboy, his Eastern European accent is very endearing and I warm to him instantly. I cannot help but laugh, and agree that he has a point. Recognising he has an audience, he continues to explain his eccentric theory. 'I think we should all move in slow motion, that way we will live longer.' He now has my full attention. 'When I go on holiday I always walk backwards, that way my holiday lasts longer.' I am now in love. 'I suppose I sound stupid,' he smiles, 'but that is not so bad.'

'I don't think you sound stupid.' I am silently quite mesmerised.

'Then maybe you are stupid too.'

I smile, 'I've been called much worse.'

'Well I figure there are more people who do not think they are stupid in the world, so if I am stupid, I am in the minority so that makes me special. I am treasured.' The twinkle in his eyes by this point is dazzling.

'I like that, we can be stupid together.' We have bonded. By this time, he is at the doorway to a supermarket where he is about to shop and I know we have to part ways, so I reach out, gently take hold of his arm and softly admit to him that he has made my day.

'I am glad, that is what I am here for, to make the world a little brighter,' and with that he disappears into the bustle of shoppers.

Bemused by our encounter, I walk around the familiar streets going over our conversation repeatedly in my head. I don't know who my mysterious stranger was or why our paths crossed in such an unexpected way but if you believe in any sort of angel, that day he was mine and now I have my answer. To live longer I have to walk backwards and back to America I have to go. I just have to find the courage to do it. What I didn't know at this stage was that my body itself would make that decision for me and give me no option if I wanted to survive. The last time I travelled across the world to America was thirty years ago, this time it will be a very different journey, and hopefully a very different outcome.

You go through life in your own space
creating places where you can linger
which make up your personal landscape,
but what happens when there is an earthquake?

CHAPTER 2

As I board the flight at Heathrow, I am relieved to be finally escaping the madness. In this busy scenario, I am invisible for all the right reasons. No one knows me or my story and I find the freedom liberating. As passengers scurry in anticipation and agitation to find their seats, I sink lower into mine and allow myself to be transported up into the unknown.

How I fell into the hands of 'those people' in the first place is perhaps irrelevant at this point but the fact that I still carry their book in my hand luggage is very telling, I can feel it watching me. Whether it is the need to distract myself from the long journey ahead or simply the discomfort of knowing the book is watching my every move, I don't know, but I recognise that the events of the past few weeks have taken their toll and maybe I should embrace this time to catch my breath. As we level into the clouds, in a desperate effort to block out the strangers around me, I think about what brought me to this place.

The silent warrior taught me that you only know what you know. I knew love and lots of it as a child but it was unexpressed, intactile, sterile love suppressed by generations of fear. My grandad's brother's body was blown in various parts over the death-stenched, mud-laden, blood poppy-coloured foreign French fields by a rifle grenade before his twenty first birthday and his tragic death accelerated the family journey into a land of fear, long before I was born. Walter, whose story will one day be well documented, is etched on every inch of my soul as clearly as his name on the war memorial outside the park gates.

My grandad set off to war shortly after, on a futile journey of his own, to avenge Walter's death and maybe bring home his dear brother's residue, but found himself caught up in the same war, only in a different country. High in the blizzard conditions of the snow-laden Italian mountains, he survived the gun fire, the horrific icy conditions and the physically, emotionally and spiritually gruelling life in the Artillery only to return home alone, without his beloved brother, without his faithful equine friend and without his soul. He removed his military jacket and used it to comfort the back of his small wooden chair in his allotment and never spoke about the war again. They sent him medals, he left them in the envelope, unopened, in the small broken down shed in his back yard and there they stayed until I found them after his death. He did not feel like a hero, Walter was the hero and Walter would wear no medals.

Life can be cruel. My grandad endured another World War as a member of the Home Guard and this time his son (my dad) was forced into this land of fear. My dad, a wonderful, gentle, affable, sweet, academic man, now adorned his own uniform of death and the war destroyed him without ever being touched by bullets. He met an angel of innocence who was sent to mend his mentally broken pieces. She was also scarred by war, losing two precious brothers so close together, one from a physically war-wounded heart and one subsequently from an alleged broken heart. Part of this angel died along with them. My dad married his angel and they clung together for safety for over fifty years until they were wrenched out of each others arms by death.

They had a child together, he was different and he died in a different way.

They suffered a painful miscarriage, a baby lost before they even saw his face.

Then they tried one last time and here I am, a result of their bravery and strength, but also a product of their fear. So afraid of losing any more, they kept me extra safe and protected out of harm's way but stifled and seeking my own safety net is what helped 'those people' to prise me away.

I wish I had known it was safe to colour outside of the lines.

An air steward bumps into my aisle seat with his trolley and jolts me back into my surroundings momentarily. Maybe at this point I should explain that I have a companion with me on my journey. He has a name but I don't use it. He is an invisible liability, a drain on my resources, a silent shadow that walks with me even in the shade. We are joined together in life and death, there is no escape. We are out of step with each other but we are inexplicably entwined. I am anxious even by the mention of his existence, so I focus on my breathing to prevent this from escalating into a full blown panic attack. It is a long, lonely twelve hour flight and although New York would have been an easier option, it is only on the West Coast that I will find my truth.

My mam passed away far too soon, my dad existed longer but never lived again. When he died, the emptying of all their possessions in the family home fell to me and me alone. I carried the burdens of the generations before me on my tired, grieving shoulders. My companion was useless and in fact hindered the grieving process and restricted my ability to cope. The poor house was waiting for my dad's return, tired and cluttered and sad. We ached together as my tears fell on the reality that the house I was born in and the family I adored, were all gone. The world never seemed so scarily colourlessness and 'those people' were nowhere to be seen. Now is my time to liberate the family fears and release the weight of all those generations of unheard voices.

Half a novel and three gossip magazines later, the journey has whittled a few more lines on my face, I have discovered that soap stars Mark and Michelle are an item and that other famous people are still, after all these years, yo-yo dieting, producing work out DVDs in their thin times and regretting it terribly when nature fights back, which inevitably it does. In a sudden urge to move the increasingly stiffening joints caused by my invisible companion, I decide to brace the turbulent walk down the aisle to the toilets. In the sanctity of this claustrophobic island of isolation, my doubts start to creep in. What am I doing? I should be in place, at home in the safety of my own space, in my own routine, instead of making regular trips to pee in mid-air because of copious amounts of water to prevent dehydrating and walking back round the long way to prevent blood clots. Despite this activity, I can feel my skin drying out and dying by the second. Catching a glimpse of myself in the toilet mirror, I quickly decide that there is little can be done to help the pale tired soul staring back at me. It is time to accept that I am just not one of those women (and there are numerous on this flight alone) who get on the plane looking like they have just stepped straight out of a luxurious pampered photo shoot for Vogue magazine and somehow after ten or twelve hours leave in the same condition. I have no idea how they do that, I content myself with the fact that it must be genetic and my genes have never been my friend. I came on this aeroplane looking fairly decent in dimmed lighting and suddenly I am at the point where I can easily scare children, not intentionally of course. Andrea Bocelli serenades me via my headphones and I drift back in time.

After my parents died, the house I was born in clung to its hoards of precious clutter, hugging it close to its chest and making me prise its contents out of its brick fingers. That was hard to do alone. I cried as I struggled to say goodbye to my past and then cried again. Eventually, the house had chance to breathe and I left it alone for a few days to give us both chance to accept it would soon have new inhabitants. When I returned, I thought the house would cry with me again but it didn't. I swear I heard it laugh as it released its past and looked forward with hope to the future with new owners, new dreams, new beginnings. The house had done its mourning, by saying goodbye to its contents, its clothes of worn furniture, tattered upholsteries, piles of read and unread books, boxes of cherished vinyl records, clothes that would not hug their owner any more, the scent of romance that once was and the last unfinished TV guide. I had arrived expecting to mourn with it but overnight it had resurrected itself with new space and new energy, giving it the will to move on. I just had to learn to do the same.

The circular wooden table where the family gathered to play games was no longer there. The wallpaper of clouds and rainbows in my bedroom, that I covered over with bright yellow paint in a moment of madness, which left my parents bemused and left me with regret. I could hear the energy and laughter of the birthday parties, the smell of the Christmas cake baking well before Christmas to let it rest, the squeaky floorboards that I knew without thinking how to avoid, the last two steps on the staircase that I rarely touched as a child, jumping over them from the third stair from the bottom, the rows of toy cars that I took through the house in a desperate race to the finish and the hook that used to hold my puppy's lead, still there, waiting. The family outtakes, the pancake that stuck to the ceiling, the stray toy that burst a pipe, the door handle that fell off and the garage key that was inexplicably missing for days.

Noisy silence. I was the only one left behind. A life of memories washed away without realising and yet I haven't lived. There were no tears. I wanted tears, but they were all gone and like the house, I must take a breath and lock the door for the last time in the hope that another somewhere is waiting to be opened. Sometimes the loudest screams are heard in the quietest whispers, unspoken sadness and unexpressed fear are deafening. My life was about to drastically change the day the clock on the wall stopped ticking because no one was left to hear it.

Suddenly the young twenty something girl next to me emerges from under her blanket and prepares for her gliding walk down the aisle. She is one of these Vogue women. Despite having just spent a couple of hours asleep with a blanket over her head, with a shake of her hair she transforms instantly to her former immaculate self. I am in awe. Needless to say my blanket remains firmly in the overhead locker, except for when I boarded the plane and some later comer decided to force a large bag into a small space and promptly deposited said blanket on to my head from a great height. That never happens to Vogue women. The young lady quickly returns and settles once more under her blanket of solitude and I drift off into another time.

I remember my frequent visits to my grandma and grandad's house. As a young child, one of my favourite things to do was to sneak into their small back room whilst the grown ups were talking and perch on my tiptoes, gazing with innocent wonder into my own eyes, which reflected back to me through the plain mirror hanging by a tarnished chain, on the tired wall. It was my entrance to Narnia, a crystal ball into my future.

In the magical abyss of my seven year old eyes, I saw a road map consisting of hundreds of tiny lights all leading to different places but all connected in an eternal circle attached to the pupil of my soul. This was my future, illuminating major interstates, minor roads, country paths and pebble tracks, all roads never yet travelled but filled with anticipation of destination. Interstate or motorway, it doesn't really matter, ultimately we are all differently the same. Somewhere down those roads awaited travel to exotic places, a career, a family and obviously a handsome knight in shining armour keeping the roads safe. I couldn't wait. There were so many questions. Where will I go? What will I do? Who will I become? The reflection staring back at me was dazzlingly optimistic. I hoped it involved a desk, paper and pens because I loved writing and I hoped I changed people's lives for the better. That was all I asked for. Before the adults missed me, I waved goodbye to my future self and crept back unnoticed into the other room. I was a healthy, athletic, imaginative child with a rainbow spirit that contagiously affected others, but I had no idea how to show it.

The mirror gazing continued for several years, although I had to invent new excuses for going into the back room as I grew older. But very gradually the light began to fade, my grandma and grandad died and I lost my secret mirror. That same day I lost my reflection and without realising I lost my focus, and blindly gave myself away, devastating my personal landscape. The road map was left crumpled in my wake and I entered the monochrome world that was to be a catastrophic landscape. When you become disjointed in such a way, infection creeps in and the bones deform, opening ravines of pain down which all of your hopes and dreams disappear, as you lose yourself either in physical or symbolic suicide. Both are equally destructive and deadly, not only to you but potentially to the sacred spaces of those around you. That's when my invisible companion arrived and deformed my body as he had my grandma's and my dad's, they call him rheumatoid arthritis or RA for short. That's when 'those people' found me, vulnerable and alone and offered me the world, but unbeknown to me it was a whole new world of pain, fear and control. Now, I need to break the cycle and make my own trail to recover the abandoned road map.

CHAPTER 3

The flight itself is a lengthy one and although the reading, movies, eating very suspicious-looking airline food and people watching take some minutes away, there are enough hours remaining to start thinking about my downward spiralling existence. I have never got used to being alone but I am learning how to deal with it. A few years ago I nearly got married again, to Daniel but he turned out to be a suicidal depressive nightmare and I consider myself to have had a narrow escape. Looking back now, as my mind appears to be desperately searching for subjects to occupy the time, I can understand his problems and hope someone has found the energy to help him through them, but he too was a victim of the brainwashing of 'those people'. That was the beauty of our brief but intense relationship and also the downfall: we were both victims. We found solace in each other and at the same time couldn't bear the mirror image. I hope he has escaped 'those people' but the last time I spoke to him, he hadn't and I have a feeling he never will.

Slight turbulence rocks my subconscious and I take a brief look at blanket head lady who is still ensconced in her dream world, before I am transported back to my nightmare world. That fateful night, I remember being tired, well, more tired that usual. The doorbell rang and at the same time there was a hammering on the door, I remember because it made me jump. A glance at the time on my phone told me it was nine fifteen and it unnerved me to have visitors at what was to me, late at night. Peeking through the small distorted glass panel on the door, it was too dark to see any familiar shadows and I hesitated before taking a deep breath and opening the door (it never occurred to me that I could have ignored it. I learned that skill later, much later). Outside stood two unwelcome faces. It was 'those people'. For the first time in my life, I almost refused to let them in but it is a fine line between being rude and assertive and I hadn't found it yet. They begged me to let them enter and I resorted to type. I regretted that decision immediately. Bland meaningless pleasantries followed for what seemed like an age and then one of these two 'sisters' uncovered the elephant in the room.

'We have new local leaders, they are the best yet.'

Well that's not saying much, I thought to myself, but civility held me back from expressing myself, among many other things. I hated how defensive I became but I was feeling passively attacked.

'Do you know one of them is my son?' she continued, oblivious of my discomfort.

'That's nice.' The phrase came out of my mouth, but my mind was thinking that her son was not about to revolutionise the organisation, everyone knew that this family just kept going by peer pressure, if only they could have all been honest with each other, the whole family could have been saved from this needless charade. 'Well that's over for me now,' I threw in for good measure in a feeble attempt at assertiveness and a hope to end the painful stilted conversation.

'Oh well, I don't like it most of the time but I go for the grandchildren.'

And there we have it. She had admitted it herself. I struggled with the insanity of the comment. The children attend for their parents, the parents attend for their children, the grandparents attend for their children and their grandchildren and everyone remains miserably caught in the wasps' nest of unhappiness. The masquerade of being a good example involves everyone living a lie and allowing future generations to suffer the same fate too. Isn't that crazy? Is it just me? There are no words. Her companion offered comforting nods of agreement at this point and then the conversation changed to irrelevant drivel. I couldn't take any more. The conversation was so grey that I wanted to throw colours at it as it passed my ears, but I had none to give.

'Well it was lovely of you to visit but it is getting late.' A polite way of saying I hoped they would get the hell out as quickly as possible. It seemed to work, they made their excuses and with a final pitying glance they left.

I collapsed against the back of the closed door in relief. Anger took over. How dare they descend on me with no warning, just wanting to see me pale, ill and crying into my lonely sinful hands. But the anger was relatively short lived. I was programmed, I scanned the room to see if it looked 'sinful'. The Christmas tree was in place, neatly decorated with the required lights and even had a star on top, they would have seen that. There was the required framed photograph of the white and spacious building they idolised in a corner of the room and my small apartment was enhanced by plentiful Christmas cards (although mostly were from people I rarely saw and long lost relations) so at least there was some semblance that my life was in order. Thank goodness. I was relieved. It was a few minutes before I realised that it didn't actually matter, I no longer had to please 'those people'. Old habits die hard and I made a mental note to try and forgive myself for this minor indiscretion, but forgiving myself was and is, still a work in progress.

Just as I was recovering from the whole nightmare experience, I noticed in my peripheral vision a small gift bag hidden down by the side of the chair. My heart sank, 'secret Santa', an old missionary tool. It was with great trepidation that I tentatively looked inside and gently unwrapped a thin layer of red tissue paper. A badly made hand-painted wooden sign which simply read 'FAITH' emerged from its hiding place. So many emotions hit me simultaneously. There was a time I would have found it endearing and hung it on the wall with pride because although it was tacky, it was made with love for me, by a friend, or so I thought. Now it glared at me like a silent assassin, a threat, a cheap jibe implying that they thought I had been led astray. The only explanation for my behaviour was loss of faith, in their blinkered eyes and now they had invaded my privacy to remind me. How dare they? My anger was resurfacing. I contemplated returning the gift to its rightful owner but I could already hear the responses: 'It was an innocent gift, but maybe we have touched a nerve, dear.' Or maybe the old: ' We were inspired to know that this is the gift you needed.' Was I simply paranoid and it really was just a thoughtful gesture? My gut feeling was that they were telling me to repent or die. This is the dichotomy of 'those people', how do you explain to people that you feel threatened by kindness? Well officer, I wish to report a crime of... gift giving.

Hidden inside the bag was a Christmas card and I knew these women were not prolific Christmas card writers. In fact notoriously, they would send one card to everyone and place it on the notice board with a message stating that any money saved by this gesture would be donated to charity. Undoubtably a noble act, but I always wondered if this ever actually happened, or was it simply a great way to save money and at the same time provide an excuse that no one would question. I would never know. Glancing at the card, a big sigh left my body as I saw the words, 'Follow the Star' written above an overtly religious scene, along with a biblical quote from Luke. It might as well have flashed 'SINNER' in neon lights. Instinctively, I threw both objects in the kitchen bin, taking solace that at least I had the wisdom to do that and I waited for the bin to disintegrate in a righteous explosion but it didn't happen, so I figured the gods weren't totally against me.

Little did I know that the gods were rooting for me in quite a dramatic way.

If you had told me that night that I would be making this journey today, I would have thought you were crazy, but my world was tilting on its axis and I recognised this as my only chance to change the direction of my life in a radical way. Waves of anxious nausea intermingle with brief (very brief) euphoric thoughts, 'what an exciting adventure' my head is saying, but my body is screaming at me that I am making a big mistake. I am too far away from my comfort zone. Loneliness is a blessing and a curse and there is a very narrow tightrope that hangs between the two places. I have fallen off a few times, usually to the dark side but I am trying to improve my balance. You are not always alone when you are lonely.

There is a point in life and over the Atlantic where you stop looking back and start to look forward to the destination ahead and I put the doubting thoughts behind me as I try to embrace the pending adventure of landing, customs and beyond. Land starts to appear and down below I see the tops of houses of unseen families and family drama, turquoise swimming pools in neatly orchestrated suburban havens. Through the tiny glass window, the heat of the sun warms my hopes of finding not only the answers I seek, but also some of the questions. I breathe a sigh of relief that I am soon going to be back on terra firma, but I am also anxious that these are my first real footsteps in life. There is a universal truth, that we all symbolically begin and end up in the soil, so on a mission to search for truth, it only seems right to learn to dance one step at a time on solid ground. Literally, figuratively, metaphorically or symbolically, I am travelling home.

LAX is a beehive of activity, ironically for a non beehive state. Everyone is focused on their own journey, whether it be arriving or departing, checking, verifying, deporting, accepting, ensuring, securing, crying, laughing, case shunting, relative hunting, peacefully or anxiously and of course there is the occasional clown, confetti bombing celebrities to the delight of the paparazzi. I need a taxi, some edible food and a comfy bed in that order, to help me acclimatise to the hectic city pace that is Los Angeles. My final destination, Hollywood, is the ideal place to study deceit. A car ride slow dance through congested traffic ends with arrival at my hotel, who awaits to embrace me like an old lover and I am ready to fall into his arms.

**'Every human thought and action
are based in love or fear.'**
Native American wisdom

CHAPTER 4

After a good night's sleep enhanced by exhaustion, enveloped in some luxurious voluptuous white cotton bedding and with the noise of jet engines still ringing in my ears, I wake re-energised but afraid of my reality. Attempting to shake off the fear, I remind myself that I am anonymous here, they cannot touch me. I take a deep breath, prise myself from this giant marshmallow of comfort, shower, dress and head out of my hotel room towards the breakfast area, trying to look like it is the most natural thing in the world, something I do all the time.

My boutique Hollywood hotel is simple and quirky. The breakfast area is not a separate dining room but an informal collection of tables and chairs and reclining couches, in a small area set aside as part of the reception space. Initially it feels wrong and bizarre, but there is something about the informality of it that is challengingly inviting to me. Taking a deep breath, I recognise the need to act like a normal human and choose my breakfast from a modest array of cereal, fruit, yoghurt, muffins and pastries and I am so overly self-conscious that it proves a difficult task. My internal dialogue has a party, what am I least likely to drop, or spill all over myself and everyone else? Will they think me unhealthy if I choose the wrong thing? Is everyone watching because I appear to be alone, or because my movements are restricted? My silent companion smirks in satisfaction that he has this affect on me and no one knows the pain.

I am starving, but in a panic of indecision pick up a single cereal bar and a minute glass of fresh orange, my thinking being that the bar can be sneaked into my bag if I don't have the courage to eat it in public and then I only have to keep an eye on the smallest glass of juice imaginable. Subconsciously, I am still slightly panicking by the fact that I have made such a drastic leap abroad with no certainties that I will find the answers I crave, and now I am sitting like the proverbial duck feeling as though all the spotlights of Hollywood are pointed at me. In addition, I now have to eat in public, in an informal setting surrounded by potential murderers, thieves, rapists or maybe just businessmen and tourists. My mind is in total paranoia mode.

The assigned breakfast eating area is fairly busy but I find a couple of seats vacant near a window overlooking Beverly Boulevard and I claim them as my own. Biting the bullet, I unwrap the alleged nutritious blueberry cereal bar in an effort to look health conscious, but inwardly I gaze longingly at the vast array of breakfast muffins. It couldn't be, I convince myself, imagine the crumbs and the look of disdain by those elegant Vogue women, what a disgrace I would be, so I try to look smugly content with my small bar of health. To be honest, my cereal bar doesn't look too healthy. It contains a lot of sugar and tastes of cardboard with the odd synthetic blueberry. I probably should have chosen the Raisin Bran or fruit but they are way too precarious to eat in public, so I acknowledge my destiny and sip my tiny juice feeling vulnerable sitting here on my own, on view to the world of couples and families. At least from my vantage point near the window I can keep an eye on Justin, the very efficient and immaculate receptionist who seems to have remembered the name of every guest, including mine, which is extremely impressive and slightly unnerving to me.

Derek, the bell hop (do they still get called that? I am tempted to say bell boy but he is one of the few people older than me) is in charge of the area between the kerbside and the reception desk and he too is fully in control. Ordering taxis, directing traffic, helping impatient travellers with their bags and despite this, finding quiet moments to join me in the breakfast area.

'You are having a busy day,' I observe, struggling to be naturally social.

'Yes, I think that is the early morning rush over.' He is a small jovial man, very smartly turned out in his navy uniform and his peaked cap. He gestures to the seat next to me. 'May I join you?'

'Of course.' I am delighted to have company even if it was only until the next guests arrive (or leave). I don't want to look as though I am alone. I am a dichotomy, craving company, but fearful of people. As he sits down, he sighs as though he is glad to give his feet a rest and takes off his hat whilst wiping his forehead with his white handkerchief.

'You are English, right?'

'Yes,' is my simple reply.

'Where in England do you live?'

I have my stock answer ready. 'The north, nearer Scotland than London.' This usually deflects the conversation about what London is like and avoids the reality that I dislike the grey capital. There is something really sweet about him, not just his slight accent, but something else, maybe it is the smile that never leaves his face.

'Aah, you know Liverpool?'

'I live nearer to Liverpool than London but I haven't been there.'

'My son, he supports Liverpool, he likes the soccer.'

'Oh yes, Liverpool are an okay team to support if you don't support Middlesbrough.' Sometimes I can't help myself. I look for a reaction in his eyes but it appears my home team are invisible to him. 'Do you like soccer?' I ask to regain my confidence.

He explains that he is originally from Brazil, the home of soccer but he supports Arsenal because he has a son who lives in London. He asks me about Middlesbrough F.C. I ramble an explanation that Middlesbrough, not too long ago used to play the likes of Arsenal and Liverpool but I sadly accept that he is an unbeliever and only interested in the Premier League, which is for my team sadly a distant memory (Although I am pleased to say the Boro have now retaken their place in the top league). At least he is not a Manchester United fan. Without much warning, a car full of guests arrives and he is called quickly back to duty and makes his humble apologies. I am alone again.

I suddenly feel like I am actually in Los Angeles. It is in the air. The Goodwill donation centre over the road is still sleeping and its neighbour TacoBell looks like it has a hangover, but it isn't nine thirty yet, Los Angeles is dreaming. A few minutes later and the sun rises from its bed to make a dramatic statement, then as though it has been caught unprepared, retreats embarrassed back under the fluffy covers, just for a little while. A school bus chuckles as it drives past.

Derek pops back in to keep an eye on the plasma television which illuminates the wall by updating anyone who is passing on the latest traffic news and gives updates on the shooting in Vegas, the missing Navy Seal and the mystery of the body in the water tank. The American Dream. A street banner for the Ahmanson Theatre waves its arms in the gentle breeze from its tethered lamppost stretching its arms to advertise The End of the Rainbow and maybe it is. The American Dream appears mortally wounded, and who knows what lies at the end of this rainbow. I see my image staring back at me through the window and I look away.

Be careful of the shards of broken glass from my reflection - if you cut yourself you will bleed like me.

What can I achieve by being here? I need a plan. Los Angeles is my starting point. Originally it made sense to head for Salt Lake City, however I have been there before and I know what I will find, stonewalling suits. 'Those people' even arrested a homeless man recently for trying to start a conversation, so what chance did I have? No, there will only be doors slammed in my face and any windows of opportunity will need to be bulletproof. I will find no answers there.

It is a sign of serendipity to me that I am in this particular area of Hollywood. There is an energy that appeals to me and only when I see the innocuous warehouse building strides from my hotel room do I understand why. Magic happens here in unusual, unexpected places. Special magical talent that is witnessed by the few but appreciated by the masses and comes at one hell of a cost in that you lose yourself to your audience. People walk past the end of this alley oblivious to the secluded space where Michael Jackson allegedly recorded his 'Thriller' album, which changed the course of his life and ours. Regardless of your taste in music, certain moments hang in the air, Michael Jackson had vision and Hollywood loves creating the impossible. Who else could successfully convince the Los Angeles authorities that he could orchestrate actual street gangs in Skid Row, to meet in up in one peaceful place, to experience together an impressive thunderclap of expression for his 'Beat It' video? This is a place that helps you achieve what you were told was impossible. Extremely ordinary from the outside but holds its secrets close to its chest, and secrets are why I am here. If you dig hard enough, shrouded secrets will be unveiled, because a secret is never yours alone, long after you have gone it will emerge and make its run for freedom. A secret that has been evolving for a long time like the charades of 'those people' will suddenly burst for freedom like a Fourth of July firework display and those involved will have to go down in the sparks or make a futile run for cover. Some secrets are destructive and dangerous, but their secrets are now leaking through these streets, yet not everyone can see them.

Los Angeles is the perfect starting point, far enough from Salt Lake to feel safe but still connected. It is Salt Lake's naughty cousin.

CHAPTER 5

Charlie Fox is busking outside the Le Brea Tar Pits when I first bump into him. I know instantly we have some connection but I am not sure what. Charmed by my accent, this antithesis of all things American strums his banjo and woos me with an endearing version of 'Mud Mud Glorious Mud', in honour of my Englishness. He doesn't realise how far from England my soul is, but I play the part and join in the chorus with him, hoping no one is watching my embarrassing participation, as the iconic, surreal, bubbling hot tar gurgles in the background.

Charlie Fox has been playing his banjo for more than fifty years and every second of that experience is tattooed on the tips of his fingers making melodic folk and blues sounds. His voice portrays the emotion of every sentence, that's why I am drawn to him, he has a story to tell and I want to read the gritty truth. I have a need for truth and this lovely man offers his truth to me through his banjo strings. Although our meeting is fleeting, I am sure to 'follow him to the hollow' and 'wallow' in the truthful tar pits. A generous tip is the least I can do for my flirtatious serenade and as I hand him a very generous layer of bills (considering I am a Yorkshire girl) he quietly pulls me towards him and whispers to me, 'Don't forget to follow the real you.' He then hands me a small tarnished circular plastic token. He explains that someone has dropped it in his banjo case and he knew instinctively that it has to go to right person, who is, apparently, me. It isn't what I was expecting but I take it politely, although I am not sure what it is and we say our goodbyes. Placing the disc in my pocket to examine later, I wander around the landscape taking in the smell of the tar and educating myself on the topography of this very unusual place.

Charlie's landscape has many scars, internally and externally. The asphalt lake of black oily gold screams at the torture of the trapped souls of animals and humans alike. This tautological place (it literally means 'the the tar tar pits') is duplicitous in its name and nature. It was once such a useful area for the native Chumash and Tongvra to live, using the natural resources available to them for making a living, the tar proved invaluable for waterproofing and sealing their redwood boats allowing them access to the Channel Islands, but eventually it became an area exploited and destroyed in an all too familiar scenario, taken from everyone as a consequence and only now, like me, it is finding a voice. The bubbling tar is telling its story and unearthing its soulful secrets. Palaeontological treasures are coming forth from the molasses tar pools (perhaps Michael Jackson was on to something with the coming forth of souls and zombies but maybe the uncreative take things too literally).

The land around has changed over the years, wild animals which once roamed this ancient city are now long gone, buried in a mound of history and fable, along with

TRAIL OF
FEARS

the people, but the tar pits are truthful, they give up their facts. Millions of handpicked bones and fossils from a variety of animals such as sabre toothed cats, camels, mastodons, and horses are carefully and methodically researched and documented. The skeletal heads of hundreds of dire wolves speak to me from their display wall, looking like an artistic Nike trainer advertising display, confirming that the wolves have left their footprints on this land. They are teaching me something. I can feel them spiritually reclaiming their landscape.

But it is not a comfortable co-existence. Everywhere I tread, the souls of my feet burn with the guilt of trespassing on this hallowed ground. I am an interloper, every pebble and blade of grass holds the energy of those who passed this way before and this land has been fought over and turned over from the beginning. My toes vibrate to their own 'Trail of Tears' and the responsibility of not abusing its trust, lies heavy in my heart. I want to help this land to heal but instead this land is helping me to realign my own personal landscape and giving me the benefit of its pain. The raven watches from its panoramic perch, flexing its atramentous wings and I am grateful.

At a conveniently placed bench overlooking the skulls, I sit down to ponder the situation. Suddenly, I remember the token, so I take it out of my pocket to examine it. Initially I thought it was just a plain circular disc but on further scrutiny it has the serenity prayer embossed on one side. The words speak to me as if this is first the first time I have heard them:

'God grant me the serenity to accept the things I cannot change, Courage to change the things I can and Wisdom to know the difference.'

In an unlikely museum, facing a wall full of wolves' skulls, I am given the purpose of my journey in simple terms. My displaced native advisors have literally spelled out their vision for me in a display that I can understand. Trying to change 'those people' is a waste of my time, energy and health, especially if they are unwilling to change. My progress should not be hindered by their reluctance to progress on the path and I am ready to move on. A lack of confidence and belief in myself can no longer stop me from doing the one thing I now know is essential in order to preserve myself. I need to walk away, not just physically but mentally and spiritually. Flipping the coin over, the phrase, 'To thine own self be true' shines out at me like a neon Vegas light. I must believe and trust in myself. I am on the right track. The earth is opening up its story and the voices that are only heard in the distant winds are speaking to me. A lesson learned not only in the mind but a lesson to be felt in the heart. Gratitude fills my soul. In geology as in life, no landscape is permanent. The round token reminds me that nature wants things to be round, to be inclusive, all to be equal and all deserve equal respect. I gave 'those people' more respect than I gave myself until I had nothing left to give anyone. My circle is broken.

This is the day I wake up. The raven flaps its midnight wings and takes off into the distance. As I leave, I look over to where Charlie had previously been wooing the never ending parade of visitors, but he has gone. People disappear so easily.

CHAPTER 6

Sunday. The day of rest from weekday labours. The outside world seems to agree with me, especially in Hollywood. The work day buzz has silenced and people are planning trips to the coast to blow off the week day stress. I am going to join them. Maybe the ocean will give up her secrets, because even this Sabbath jaunt would be frowned upon by 'those people'.

A sweaty, meandering forty five minute Metro bus ride later and I am standing on the beach at Santa Monica. Mesmerised by the beauty, I give in to the natural urge to stand barefoot on the inviting grains of sand. What is it that makes me want to stare into the ocean all day? There is a vision of infinity as its magnetic forces pull me inwards, giving me the desire to walk right into its heart and either drown in the solitary silence of this underwater world, or rise above it and ride the energy of the waves.

Either way, one important commodity is required: surrender. It is one of those misunderstood words that appears to be very negative and weak but actually is extremely powerful and strong.

Sometimes it is good to surrender meekly and in the true essence of the words of Paul McCartney, 'let it be.' That statement can so easily be misunderstood.

First of all, do not misinterpret 'meek' as 'weak', but rather to be open, with no ego. Secondly, the absence of ego, the giving up, in a healthy way, any control we think we have (which of course we don't) is strength at its very core. I can hear 'those people' saying maybe I should 'let it be' but they don't understand the words. 'Let it be' does not mean let the pain invisibly continue, however convenient that may be.

I realise that deep down I am still angry. I walk further along the beach, feeling the soft warm sand between my toes, and the invitation to sink into the earth is too strong to resist and I let myself fall slowly down on to the sandy bed, with great pain, no help from my invisible companion and little dignity. But the effort is worth it as this is the closest thing to relaxing I have done in a long time. I lie back and watch the gulls waltzing overhead and the word 'bliss' crosses my mind, but it is only for a brief moment as I shake the thought away as though it is the procrastination of a naughty schoolgirl avoiding her homework. Slightly reluctantly, I take my favourite black pen and my baggage-weary notebook out of my small canvas shoulder bag and fulfil the need to focus. The blank page talks to me:

Who was Joseph?
What is true?
How do I find the elephant?

Maybe I have become distracted in my search for truth, yet by doing so I may have come nearer to it. The sun, the ocean, the energy have caused me to forget the smaller inconsequential things. Is that a good thing? Perhaps they are all distractions. The truth is big and important. I add the question:

How do I change this black and white world into colour?

'Those people' say to be careful of putting your trust in man and yet they manipulate you in order to get your trust and that confuses me. Was Joseph confused? Well, I guess he was just another person like us and he was trying to get through life the best way he knew. I am no longer sure who he was, a Prophet, a wise man or a foolish man, a trickster, a deliberate deceiver, a charlatan, a con man, an honest man or a dishonest rogue. Whatever or whoever he was, he paid with his life, but then eventually we all do.

This is half the problem, we come into this life alone and we leave it alone, but being alone scares people, fear of the unknown scares people, and so what better way to manipulate than to threaten (in a passive aggressive way) that if you doubt or disbelieve or disobey, you will be alone forever. Your family and friends will be separated from you in the eternities, as well as in this mortal life, as you are cast aside like a leper. They will be actively encouraged to disown and disassociate with you, so for most members the odds are stacked too high and so they fold. Prophet or profiteer?

The healing heat of the day helps me to reflect on just how innocently vulnerable I was when 'those people' first entered my world and set the spider's web, but my daydreaming is suddenly interrupted by a shaft of sunlight falling on my page and creating a grey prism. I read that as an acknowledgement that all will be well and I am on the right trail. Press forward old saints. Surrounded by beautiful dry powdery sand, it suddenly occurs to me that maybe to dig up the dirt, I need to go to the desert, where I am sure many entered but few came out unscathed, there is a reason why, *A Study in Scarlet* by Arthur Conan Doyle is not on certain bookshelves. I realise this is my first glimpse of the elephant.

I need the healing heat of the desert. I am still in recovery, physically, mentally and emotionally. The only sign I had was severe anaemia, literally the life blood drained out of me. The resulting drama is painful to recount even now to myself, but I go over the edited version in my mind. A young doctor with panic etched on his face tried to explain how it was a miracle that I was still conscious and that I needed an urgent blood transfusion. I knew instinctively when the first blood transfusion didn't work that I was in trouble but luckily I didn't know how much. Another blood transfusion caused a dispute between medical staff. Is that where I was infected with shingles? Is that possible? They disagreed with each other but whatever the truth, I had shingles all over the left side of my face.

The next day, after an allergic reaction to the medication they gave me for the shingles, my face was so distorted I looked ironically, considering my current search, like the elephant man. I had never felt so ill and so out of control. They placed me in the bed on the corner of the ward where in my desperate state I saw the pitiful look of the other patients and visitors. I remember the looks on their faces, especially the younger ones who stared and asked 'what was wrong with that lady', but were told to be quiet and rushed away. Those moments helped me to realise how we do not know how to react to anybody who is different, even though I believe most humans do at some level, with their heart, but they don't know how to tell their faces or mouths. I would have been the same. Then a few days later I remember telling the nurse I couldn't stop shaking, apparently a forty one degree temperature does that to you. It was ten o'clock at night and the doctor had gone home. I heard the nurse frantically asking for his advice on the telephone. A wonderful elderly patient in her eighties came over and started massaging my arms and face. It was the most beautiful feeling in the world. In every day life I generally dislike being touched by strangers, but there in this seemingly life or death moment, the touch of another human was all I craved. It was serenely beautiful, and took me mentally to a place away from fear, a very spiritual surreal place that I can't explain, but I will be eternally grateful to her for recognising this unspoken need. However, she was instantly told by a rather severe nurse to step away and not touch me for fear of cross infection. Luckily for me this angel was feisty and not only ignored the direction, but after asking me if I wanted her to stay (which of course I did) told the nurse if she wanted to remove her, she would have to do so physically. The nurse sighed in angry frustration and decided her time was better spent trying to get the doctor to come back to the hospital. Bless the doctor, as he did just that. I heard the phrase 'her kidneys have shut down' and I remember someone talking to me about kidney failure but it was through a haze of clouds. The doctor was anxiously deciding which treatment to give me and tried to organise a fan to blow cold air on me to get my temperature down, but was told by a nurse that fans were banned on the ward for fear of cross infection. I remember his disbelief and I noted that 'cross infection' must have been the new buzz word and if I could have spoken I would have said, 'let's turn down the heating, open some windows and allow visitors to cheer the place up with flowers. We all seem to be sick here anyway so your sterile cross infection rules are not working.' But what did I know? I was sick.

Luckily for me, the nurse agreed that it seemed a severe disadvantage not to have a fan to hand so she came up with the ingenious idea of filling a pillowcase with ice cubes for me to cuddle, to see if that helped. I was willing to try anything by this time so it seemed a good idea. It turned out to be blissful relief. I hugged the life out of that pillowcase and promptly with the help of intravenous drugs, fell into a deep sleep.

Waking up the next day was as big a shock to me as to the doctor who saved my life. His eyes lit up when he saw me, as he was expecting the worst, but I felt amazingly well considering. He explained that the kidneys had stopped working for no obvious reason and in the same way had, thank goodness, suddenly started again. The whole experience taught me that doctors don't have all the answers but they certainly try their best, and the following conversation we had is as vivid today as it was then: 'Whatever stress is in your life, you need to eliminate it, because that is the only thing that I can think of that made this situation so severe.' This was his unofficial diagnosis. The only stress in my life was 'those people' and my life was centred around them, I explained. 'Then change your life and leave those people, for the sake of your health,' he replied.

That is when my eyes really opened for the first time. It was such an unbelievable concept that it jolted me into the reality of the sad truth. I was incredibly physically and spiritually dehydrated and this wonderful doctor had taught me how to hydrate myself with the water of life. That was the day I started in my search for truth and it opened up a whole new way of life.

An inquisitive seagull enquires into the contents of my bag, bringing my mind back to the beach and I gently shoo it away. I have no food, so it is out of luck anyway, but as I repack the disturbed contents of my bag, I am reminded to add another layer of sun cream to my lower legs as they peep out from my rolled up jeans and I realise I have been here a while. I don't like to wear sun protection but before you bombard me with judgement, I am thoroughly overdressed with all other extremities covered. Yes, baring your shoulders or wearing anything above knee length is another sin and one at the moment I am in no danger from.

I pull my rebellious baseball cap further over my face and remember that I was in my twenties when I first encountered the missionaries and I was quickly labelled 'the golden child'. This was a phrase given to converts who 'got it' straight away, someone who embraced the teachings immediately and I swallowed it hook line and sinker. It wasn't a case of 'if' I got baptised but 'when'. I was searching to fit in, looking for my identity and life was hard particularly since my invisible companion had just turned up, ending my athletic youth. They taught that life is a trial and the bad times are to test our faithfulness and for which we would be rewarded in the good times. Such a test appealed to my competitive nature, I liked a challenge and they made bad experiences sound like a series of exams which the perfectionist in me wanted to pass. The icing on the cake or ironically the cream in the coffee was the fact that like me, they didn't drink tea, coffee or alcohol. This was music to my caffeine-resistant taste buds. There were suddenly more people like me, I put on my metaphorical dance shoes and danced those baptismal blues. I took my baptismal promises very seriously, became what is known in the business as a TBM (True Blue/Believing Mormon) and dedicated the next thirty years to everything they taught me. I was obviously too faithful for my own good, there were plenty of warning signs which I rationalised away because we were taught from the pulpit every week that any doubts we expressed were simply an indication of our lack of faith and clearly more scripture study was required. It was a real life, *Emperor's New Clothes* scenario. Everyone repeating their indoctrinated mantra like the robots they were, and despite my staunch obedience, I never fit in.

Promoted as a family-orientated church, the truth is that the goal of every single member is under the strict patriarchal order to marry into a 'good church family', which means that they are still casting their net not far from the polygamy idea, that for all my church life was dismissed as a vicious rumour. The bigger the church family, the more secure you are in the programme and the more impossible it will be to escape, but they leave that bit out. This also means that you are not supposed to date outside the organisation also for fear of being led astray, but of course that also is a means of control. The men are in charge, make no mistake about that, so a divorced woman with an invisible health companion is the lowest on the pecking order. The fact that I accepted this, shows how low my self-esteem has fallen. But they used my divorce against me and labelled me unfairly as a bitter divorcee with an axe to grind against men which is unbelievably untrue, but it provides them with a 'get out' clause and allows them to rationalise my fall from grace in their eyes, as being my own fault. The rapist's victim is subject to discipline for 'disobeying' their honour code and I should know.

Memories drained and exhausted, I relax and let my mind wander the waves enjoying the comfort of the warm sandy beach and look out into the largest body of water I have ever seen, in fact I am amazed such an ocean exists. Growing up near the grey North Sea, I always thought that maybe blue water was an optical illusion in photographs and never really happened, but here it is, a picture book body of water, with wonderful breaking waves which look more inviting than anything I have ever seen. It is not long before I cannot resist the urge to dive in and taste the water. When I say 'dive' in, I mean paddle up to my knees. I still have my hang ups about exposing my body but you can't undo such teaching easily and my invisible companion hates physical activity.

There are plenty of young bikini-clad bodies toned to perfection mingling with those slightly older more realistic bodied folks, like myself, all in various depths of deep surf-inducing water. For some, even in California, it is too cold and they dip a toe in and run back to their friends, others literally dive in head first and get the cold shock over with in one sudden movement and look very cool to their peers and observers like me in the process. Just as in life itself. Despite my being a toe in the water type adult, mainly because of 'those people', my inner child is a dive in the deep end girl but fear makes you cautious. The water itself is not an obstacle for me, I swam like a fish before and my body remembers, even though it won't replicate and once you have paddled off Redcar beach, you fear no water, whatever the temperature. Gazing over the crashing waves to the horizon you get a glimpse into eternity. This is the message Santa Monica is repeating to me. The destination will take care of itself, but don't lose yourself to the luggage labels along the way, stay true to the person deep down you know you are. Charlie's token shines in agreement in my pocket. I think it is like getting a train, it doesn't matter which train you choose as long as it is going to the place you want to arrive at and not the place everyone else is telling you to go to.

Then it suddenly dawns on me that I actually see it is blue. I saw it with my mind and it passed by unnoticed, but after feeling its breath, I can feel the colour unwinding and relaxing my heart. The ocean is beautiful cobalt blue with a wonderful, white crescendo topping. Suddenly I can breathe, I mean really breathe, the wind of wisdom is showing me the north and south of colours and peace, trust and innocence are words dancing on the water.

I splash around in the first glimpse of colour in years, like a child in wellies on a puddle-riddled path. I dance like the famous disabled pigeon in the dancing fountain on Middlesbrough's Boulevard. Yes, Middlesbrough has a famous one-legged pigeon and yes, Middlesbrough has a Boulevard, I know, my mother named it. She had tea with the Mayor, and my dad tried on his robes, it was a proud day for them. Anyway, I digress. The ocean communicates with me via the foam-ridden galloping stallions and explains that the truth of the waters of baptism are clear but the dirt lies in the antithesis of the desert. To find my truth I have to face my demons head on and go to the dehydrated landscape that has learned to maintain fluid balance. The trail to the elephant is across the Mojave Desert and into Las Vegas. The Mormon Corridor. The counterfeit Bible belt.

A seagull bows in front of me and releases a white feather.

The truth lies in the deceit
I went to the place where they both did meet

CHAPTER 7

Interstate 15 knows my name. I don't know why but I can see it written in the tarmac. It is a road with possibilities. Stretching from the borders of Canada down through Montana and Utah to California and Nevada, making it one of the longest north south interstate highways, and with that comes knowledge, which brings a sense of immense freedom. One road with many possibilities and today it is taking me to Las Vegas.

This is the landscape that makes me feel alive. The natives consider the desert to be a healing place and I have to agree. I have heard some of 'those people' call this scenery, 'a road of nothing', but to me it is a 'road of everything'. The 'nothingness' is the Mojave desert, bare dusty rock, framed by indigo-hued mountains against a backdrop of cerulean sapphire. To those who do not see, a desert is a an empty field, but to me it is a treasure chest of shiny jewels. Each small speck of sand, rock or dust tells its own story and builds its own landscape intermittently dancing around strange iconic Joshua Tree people. Ironically the rumour has it that the mid nineteenth century settlers named this tree as it reminded them of the Biblical story of Joshua raising his hands up to the sky in prayer, now they miss the signs and see it just a rogue inkblot on an otherwise blank page.

The Lux bus taking me over this field of dreams is proving to be a friendly, comfortable companion. My seat on the front row allows more comfort for my tired legs and enables access to the views of the outside terrain. It also allows the privilege of a glimpse inside of the driver's world, although I sense from his demeanour that he is not happy. He looks tired. After we hit the interstate, he calls over the stewardess who has so far looked after us all with clipboard authority. They exchange a few words, she disappears down the bus and returns a few seconds later with a plastic cup full of nuts and a can of Coke. She places them carefully in the driver's cup holders and returns to her other duties. My suspicions appear to be validated as it looks like the poor driver is trying to stay awake, which I am all in favour of at this point. He eats the nuts one by one, trying to take off the shell with one hand whilst keeping his other on the steering wheel, which is quite a difficult manoeuvre so in the end he decides it is easier to pour the nuts into his lap, eat the nut as it is and spit the shell out into the empty plastic cup. I silently applaud his ingenuity. As he washes them down with a swig of Coke, I feel more relaxed, assured that he is more likely to stay awake and in control.

The bus is quite busy but I have a seat to myself, as does the older lady opposite me, however, on boarding she requested the assistance of a young male passenger, who dutifully obliged and lifted her luggage on to the rack above her head. As he went to make his escape to the back of the bus, she suggested he sat next to her. He seemed reluctant, but credit to his parents, he saw that she needed the company. After a couple of hours of her non-stop talking, he now either regrets his decision or he has decided that she is his surrogate granny and after the next few hundred miles they know everything about each other. She is visiting some friends in Vegas for the weekend before returning to St George. Her daughter was worried about her travelling alone on a bus but she assured her that she was more than capable of looking after herself, which she quite clearly is. He is on his way to a convention in Vegas where he hopes to get some business contacts and has some assignments to complete for some exam he has coming up on his return. It turns out that his mother's sister comes from St George and she is married to a man who comes from near where she lives, so the old lady vaguely knows of the family, a connection which delights her. For the rest of the trip, she produces sandwiches and drinks at regular intervals, which she shares with the young man and seems to enjoy looking after him. I am happy to be listening to their conversation and not have to engage in any small talk. The stewardess comes round with snacks and drinks and I am grateful for both. Unlike my older travelling companion, I have not prepared a banquet ready for the trip, but the book is still watching.

There is a pain etched on the rugged terrain, the dehydrated hopes and dreams of those who just wanted to be left alone by the elements. An hour further on from Vegas in the Moapa Valley lies the area where the

Puebloans and Southern Paiutes co-existed relatively unscathed, until 'those people' arrived in the 1800s. But their story is the ever familiar one of lives being destroyed and landscape being forever scarred in sadness. The unspeakable treatment of the Moapa people is an indication of how manipulated people can be. They were unwittingly forced into a dependency role with 'those people' who not only brought new diseases into the area but also strategically occupied water sources, reducing the ability of the indigenous people to hunt and gather natural foods, forcing these peaceful people to be no more than low paid labourers to their intruders. But then why should I be surprised? We were taught that the natives and 'those people' had a relatively peaceful co-existence and that is what I believed, despite inconsistencies in this theory, which shows the level of brainwashing.

In the book (that despite everything, I still hold near me) it states that Nephi and his descendants of Nephites (the heroes of the book) are 'white and delightsome', but if you start to be naughty like their antagonists the Laminates (who I was taught were unequivocally the Native Americans) then you will be cursed, like they were, with 'a skin of blackness' because of iniquity. Shockingly racist to read, but if you doubted it, you were chastised for clearly not being spiritual enough to see the deeper symbolic meanings.

I had never even heard of the Indian Placement Program until recently, but it ran, incredibly from 1947 to 2000. The idea of this scheme was to encourage the poor (but not troubled) natives on their reservations, who had little education and little knowledge of the sophistication of western manipulation, to hand over their children to 'those people' to be fostered and adopted into 'good families' who would teach them a new language and assimilate them into American culture, basically turning them into 'white and delightsome' children. Their parents agreed with this as it appeared an opportunity to help their children and some were so indoctrinated that they genuinely believed that their skin colour would be changed, and the 'curse of blackness' lifted for their children.

Exact numbers are elusive as are most reliable statistics for 'those people' but it has been estimated that in excess of 40,000 were involved. The confusion of their situation, their everyday life between two identities and the influences of 'those people' led many to depression and suicide and sadly many were abused. Shocking to even consider and yet the same thing is happening right now with the LGBT youth. Not is only is a gay lifestyle viewed and labelled by leaders as a 'counterfeit' lifestyle, but children of gay couples are treated differently, unequally, 'to protect them' of course, is the official line, but the current suicide numbers tell their own story. It breaks my heart and yet helps me to understand that I want no part of this reality. This is in my present day landscape and simply cannot be airbrushed away as folklore. My young optimistic self in my grandad's mirror would never have believed this lack of progress in humanity.

The transient identity of modern day Vegas, where 'outlaws' feel right at home, seems to be the crux of that delicate balance between running away and running to. This is the place where grey becomes a power of its own. The bus window suddenly unveils signs of human life as we approach a small iconic town and it shakes myself and my fellow passengers out of our daydreaming state, encouraging us to prepare for a pit stop on our desert journey.

Barstow lies fifty five miles north of San Bernardino. It is the half way point between Los Angeles and Las Vegas, nestled in the southern desert in the state of California. The Crossroads of Opportunity is its fitting motto as it is a flurry of activity in the middle of the desert as people stop either on their way to or returning from Vegas. What stories it could tell of lost fortunes and secret affairs, comforting the heartbroken and embracing those who are running away and running to. This is why I head down this part of the Corridor, it is the beginning and the end, the alpha and omega. Indirectly, I am part of that story and that is why my shadow is cast over this land. I always felt that the desert held the answers but it was the first time that I have the right questions.

The bus pulls up into the bus park to take a breath. As I step from the bus at Barstow station, I walk over to the deserted Union Pacific railway line and contemplate how far I have come. The symbolism of the railway is not lost on me, the straight and narrow path which I am all too familiar with. The tracks are ready and waiting although no trains are in sight, but it is all down to timing which is a split second of difference between life and death in the desert. I can't help but feel an analogy with the railway tracks. Previously, I was never at the right junction, perhaps I needed to re-route (who knows why I couldn't see it) but now I am ready to stop at the signals and consider my direction, opening up to the possibility that trains head in all kinds of different directions and one will eventually pass through here once again, raising eyebrows and dust in its wake. It will know where it is going even if I don't. The tracks have been laid and they are ready. Suddenly a phrase came to me that an old friend once told me: 'It is only impossible if you make it impossible', and for the first time I understand it. There is a point to this journey and it is possible to have my voice heard, I am on the right track.

The raven perched on its tree in the distance catches my glance and flies away.

The stop at Barstow is just long enough for the weary travellers to stretch their legs, use the bathroom and grab some food. Those who aren't using the time to indulge in a well needed cigarette use any spare time to purchase an overpriced memento of their visit to this iconic stop near Route 66 and I don't smoke, of course 'those people' don't allow that, so having used the facilities I am now browsing the souvenirs. Initially, I am tempted by a book on the wildlife of the desert which seems fascinating, all these picture book scorpions and rattlesnakes actually exist out there which is mind blowing to my sensitive Yorkshire soul. My practical side kicks in and so in my endeavour to travel light I decide to purchase a blue bandana with the white symbol of Route 66, to celebrate the road on which my colourful reunion started.

As I return over towards the bus, I notice that not many passengers have found their way back yet, so I walk over to the surrounding wire fencing behind the bus and gaze into the distance of the calico hills of San Bernardino County. I can image this as a one time trading post, with the hustle and flurry of people passing through and I guess in many ways nothing has changed, people are still searching for their dream. Only a few miles away, the old west silver mining towns like Calico, aptly named by the early prospectors who established them, who were so full of hope at one time back in the 1880s, only a decade later to find they had run out of luck. Leaving only ghosts to hover over the land. A century later and the destruction or progress continues as nearby Yermo, a name derived from the Spanish word for 'wilderness' stands as a prime example of wilderness cut in two by Interstate 15 and the world moves on. Two minutes later and so do we.

CHAPTER 8

As I contemplate what I am going to do in Vegas, I guess I haven't really thought about it too much. There is a comfortable hotel room with my name on it for my aching bones and more than that I have no clue. This is my modern day pioneer bus ride. After Joseph's 'murder' by a mob in Carthage Jail in 1844, 'those people' were forced out of Nauvoo, Illinois for their behaviour (or persecuted depending on your perspective) and by 1848 had forged a trail from over the Plains to the West led by Brigham Young, the new prophet, who announced that he had found the place he saw in a vision and went ahead to colonise what is now Salt Lake City.

They were not unique in this pioneering spirit, although they let you think they are, but they trekked parallel with other emigration trails of the time and followed the same routes as the Oregon and California Trails. This is where many converts from the British Isles and the rest of Europe who had been taught by missionaries in their homeland were encouraged to leave everything behind and join in this spiritual walk to Zion. Unfortunately, for these early pioneers consisting of many young families, it proved to be extremely gruelling to trek. The harsh uncharted wilderness, exposed these faithful souls to the unforgiving elements and forced them to endure much sickness and fatigue. Many died, and were simply buried by family members along the way. There was no going back, any weakness was spiritual death as this hardship was taught simply as a test to their faith. In addition, church leaders later poorly organised the various handcart companies brought in to make the trek easier, as ever being economical with the truth, disguising their ineptitude with 'revelation'.

The Perpetual Emigrating Fund was established to help the stragglers make the trip, ranking converts by their usefulness and length of church membership, but in return for the aid they were given, they were also expected to earn that money back and repay the church with interest. So there was no way to give up in the middle of the journey. These converts had given up everything to join this dream of building God's kingdom and were subtly indebted to the church and so the church owned them. The Edmunds-Tucker Act of 1887 finally helped to end this fund as part of its policy to restrict the church and their ways, including the practice of polygamy. I was taught this was all very unfair and simple persecution of very righteous saints, the polygamy rumour just being a small landscape molehill, which was a brief faux pas on behalf of a small minority of inconsequential members and we didn't need to discuss it as the church has moved on. Our bus is still moving on too and once Barstow is in the rear view mirror, the energy changes. Whether it is the excitement of my fellow bus travellers or my own anticipation, I don't know but the sense that we are approaching somewhere special is tangible and hangs in the air.

Arriving into Vegas on Interstate 15 is a surreal experience. The scenery changes suddenly from desert space and open silence, to occasional building, sporadic noise then on to the atmospheric old time Vegas and 'Billy Bob's' iconic signage. Gradually traffic increases and you can feel the excitement bubbling, laughing and partying in the air, it is tangible, it tantalises the senses into believing that something special is about to happen. The buildings move towards you faster, bigger, better and then you reach an explosion of new Vegas. Large overstated corporate clandestine hotels and casinos now compete fiercely with each other, overvalued real estate land, each trying to outshine their neighbour. People scurry like ants, moving quickly and easily between each ant hill casino. It is everything that is wrong with the world. Excess in everything. Yet it is strangely enticing, like studying a hornets' nest in amazement knowing it is compelling yet understanding there is a dangerous risk of pain from the sting in its tail.

Vegas is one big illusion, everyone in it is an illusion and so the magic lives on in this cauldron of energy. Penn and Teller shout out from their advertising poster vantage point, but at least with them you know you are being deceived. It is everything I should dislike, but Vegas is built on very detectible layers and each layer carries well documented and transparent risks, that is until you dig deep to the murderous depths of the dusty desert stones and then you hit secrets. Lots of secrets. But do that at your own risk. I am just digging in the top soil. The top layer of Vegas holds no judgement. You can forget yourself and be authentic in a place where everything is unauthentic, where anything goes and anything is possible. I like that. It doesn't necessarily mean you need to become promiscuous and deal in excess but it means you are free to be yourself and not have to look over your shoulder (unless you are guilty and then you will always look over your shoulder). What you look like, what book you live by, what you eat, where you sleep, where you spend your time, where you wake, who you kiss, who you talk to, who you are: Vegas doesn't care and won't tell you what you should be.

Ironically, it is as far away from the restrictions of 'those people' as possible and yet it was 'those people' who helped to build Vegas at the ground floor level, in those deep levels that hold more secrets than I will ever know or ever want to know and the recurring theme isn't so much that 'what happens in Vegas stays in Vegas' but rather, 'wherever there are 'those people', there are secrets'.

However, I should add that my theory falls short because it is a fake existence in this strip of land. It is as fake as 'those people' and therefore this reality can only be sustained for a maximum of three to five days depending on your stamina and constitution and then you must leave or Sin City will devour you and spit you out, just as 'those people' do. The lower layers of sand will protect Vegas from divulging any of its secrets and you don't want to be around if those sands begin to shift. There is a reason for Area 51. My stay in Vegas will be within those permitted three to five days.

The girl in my grandad's mirror used to think truth was easy to see but it has remained elusive to me. Wallace Stevens was right and I can confirm that the only time I can honestly say I have ever seen the truth was in the eye of a blackbird. I saw one lying injured and dazed in the middle of a busy road once and as I stopped the traffic to pick it up and carry it to safety, in that moment our eyes met. I realised he knew things I longed to learn. But, in the silence of the moment, he whispered, 'patience.' His recovery was quick, and he flew away fifteen minutes later, but the lesson he taught me is with me for life.

CHAPTER 9

The bus eventually pulls up in the underground car park at Harrahs Casino and there is an instant scramble amongst the passengers to be the first to depart, despite the fact that they have to wait for the driver to unload the luggage. Not wishing to be involved in such a melee and quite frankly incapable, I sit back and wait for the rush to die down. It crosses my mind that someone could take off with my small suitcase but I consider that nothing in there is irreplaceable so I take the chance. I am last to get off the bus, assisted by the lovely lady in charge of the snacks who helps me down the steps and hands me my luggage, which despite my fears has survived safe and well. I head straight to the taxi rank where a row of yellow vehicles snake through the concrete landscape, all fighting for my attention. It is with some relief that I land safely in the presence of the doorman at the MGM.

The famous golden MGM lion stands majestically in the midst of an exceptional flower display in the centre of the reception area towering over all its prey. Vegas is a jungle is full of critters like me, but the giant lion of bygone times smiles as he poses for photos from every angle. He likes the attention, I can tell. Posing in front of the lion, presumably for some promotion photos are some scantily-dressed bikinied beauties who are apparently Miss

Tropicana finalists, each vying for individual attention and each unashamedly trying outshine and out-tan their competition. I walk past the crowd they are attracting, to check in to the hotel, extremely glad for my small trusty suitcase which I push in front of me for protection as a walking aid to guide me through the unknown.

The reception area is a hustle of activity with excited guests, some checking in, some checking out, some in search of the concierge, some complaining, some celebrating, people being people. As I queue patiently in the accepted English tradition, the line moves quickly and efficiently as numerous receptionist worker bees buzz at high pace on their bee hive of a vast reception counter. Within a few minutes I am assigned a room that hopefully suits my every need. On my way back through the lobby, I cannot help but glance again at these young bikinied hopeful souls. I smile. Oh to be young again, growing up is definitely to be avoided. One minute you think you are so hip and happening, that you can change the world, but before you know it, your dodgy hips are dressed in pyjamas driving the wrong way down the A19. Life can be so cruel.

The elevators are quick and friendly. I always get the urge to put on a show for the numerous hidden cameras that I imagine are being manned 24/7 by a team of eagle-eyed security mafia, but I never do, I am too well behaved and frankly too tired and before I have chance to reconsider, my elevator ushers me out to my intended dizzy height. The endless surprisingly silent corridor invites me with the invisible companion on my shoulder to room 27-430, my home for the next couple of days. My king premier room does not disappoint, providing me with comfort, refreshments and easy access to all facilities.

This hotel is my friend, welcoming, vibrant and colourful. It never ceases to amaze me how you can be in a bustling, outrageous, noisy, smokey, people-filled casino and then seconds later be ensconced in the luxurious silence and privacy of your own room. I love both scenarios and right now I need both. My insecure self is begging me to hide under the well-pressed sheets until I can get a flight home and my liberated self is telling me to dance through the lobby naked. I need a compromise.

Out of the panoramic window I have a wonderful view of the Strip. I can just make out the Bellagio fountains entertaining like a posturing peacock, between the huddle of buildings. It is simply breathtaking. An extraordinarily large bed adorns the amply-spaced room along with an impressive writing desk and a couple of very comfortable armchairs. After examining the white, gleaming bathroom with its gold fixtures and fluffy white towels, I return to the bedroom and sit down along the spacious window ledge. I draw my knees as close to my chest as I can and press my face against the glass. If I could stay in one place forever, this would be it. I feel the glass vibrations from the noise of New York-New York rollercoaster, the distant fall of water from the Bellagio fountain show and the rumble of traffic tearing up the tarmac on the Strip, but I can't hear any of it which makes it surreal and allows me to be part of something vital and present, yet at the same time withdraw to a distance from it. That is exactly where I am at. I have lived the life I was told to for so long that now I am without a compass and I am hovering between finding the terrifying and exciting reality. In fact, I think excitement is terrifying and I make a mental note to change my thoughts on that before too long. The contrails of tiny aeroplanes write silent messages in the sky and I wonder at the vastness and majesty of life.

Time ticks by, the lengthy bus journey takes its revenge, the cotton wool cloud of a bed calls my name and I submit to it. The toll of the travel wakens my subconscious restlessness and forces me to reminisce about the first unintentionally ignored red flag with 'those people', sadly only probably eighteen months after being taken under their wing. I was taken into a room alone with a leader. He chastised me for wearing earrings. It sounds ridiculous now, but I am reliving it, although with the luxury of dream improvisation, I am telling him off and storming out. That didn't really happen of course. I told him truthfully that they were a gift from a friend. He suggested that they were no real friend and that I should sever ties with them immediately. He continued to tell me, in no uncertain terms, that I should remove the said earrings immediately and throw them away. Why? Because they were in the shape of a cross and although they believed in the crucifixion, they wanted to dwell only on the resurrection and crosses were taboo. I did what I was told. It never occurred to me that I had a choice because I was not given one. If I refused, eternal damnation was my immediate destination. Even in my dreamlike state it sounds stupid, but it was very real. It takes the happier memory of Charlie Fox's serenade to help the day fade into the night and I drift off to more pleasant places.

> **You think a paper cut hurts**
> **Until you are cut by a knife.**

CHAPTER 10

We are all 'seeking the elephant', we just don't know it. Whether your answer lies in religion, politics, work, sex, alcohol, drugs, food, fitness regimes, doing good, doing nothing, staying on the side of the law or fighting the law, guns and gangs, or family plans, we are all searching for the elephant. The problem is that the more we look, the less we find, because the elephant doesn't like noise but is found in silence, in those moments that stop us, that make us look inside the places that scare us, make us realise our own mortality. The elephant is not on the outside but the inside. Not many of us want to face that because we don't want to. We don't want to stop, we live in the iCloud rather than lay on our backs and watch the infinity of the real clouds because that would be scarily out of our control and most of us like control. Of course we are not in control of anything.

Let's go looking for my elephant.

A new day, a new start. Breakfast at Cafe 24 is a pleasant experience. Strangely, I feel less conspicuous because it is busy and the assigned table for one is tucked away in the corner out of the way. A soccer game is being shown on one of the many televisions dotted around the room, confusing many who discuss the rules of this alien sport and I smile at the knowledge that I know more about the game than several of these customers but no one would ever guess. Of course it is Vegas, so although it is breakfast for me, there are revellers of every age who clearly are still celebrating a long night but it doesn't matter, everyone is happy in their own escaped reality and it is surprisingly easy to make friends if you allow yourself the opportunity. I am working on that. There are no clocks because we don't need one, night can be day and day can be night, it doesn't matter here, we are all running from the tick of the clock and living in the spaces between. Over a two egg breakfast and a spectacular display of fresh fruit, I contemplate my next move.

Today is for research. No one believes the truth about 'those people' because they are presentable, polite, suited and booted silent assassins. The evidence is there on the internet but as members you are discouraged from using the internet as it is under Satan's control. Oh wait, forget that. The internet is now widely used as a missionary tool, both through official websites and inspirationally 'called' internet missionaries. Suddenly as the internet takes off, Satan doesn't mind sharing it any more. Warn your children nothing in life is free and theirs is one free book you do not want. However, I think it only fair that if I am doubting it, I need to internalise why. We are taught that if you ever question, all you have to do is work out that Joseph was a prophet and if that is true, the rest all falls into place. I had no problem believing that Joseph was a prophet for thirty years because of everything I was taught. Unfortunately I wasn't taught the truth, as I was about to find out in more glorious detail.

The one person who would know if Joseph was a Prophet was Emma, Joseph's one and only faithful wife, whose picture adorns all respectable Relief Society rooms. Relief Society is the women's organisation where we all strive to be like Emma. Every Sunday, the three hour church meeting is split into three sections, one being the more recognisable church service, with talks and hymns, the second being a Sunday School class for indoctrination and the third is split as the men go to their Priesthood session and the women go to Relief Society. Children attend the church service meeting and then have two hours in their own primary or youth classes, away from their parents. We are taught that the woman compliments the Priesthood holder (God forbid you might think this is a sexist organisation). The women are kept busy in Relief Society while the men make the important decisions. The three most important things in Relief Society are the picture of Emma, a table, preferably decorated with an embroidered tablecloth and flower display, and you, dressed appropriately (no shoulders exposed, nothing above calf length, no trousers, no piercings, tattoos, no wild hairstyles… even I am bored with the list now). Basically, the more immaculately groomed you are, the more important you become.

The Prophet has fellow Apostles who make up the

Quorum of the Twelve, replicating Jesus and his twelve disciples. We do what they tell us, from what to read, what movies to watch, how to dress (even down to special underwear), how to spend our time, how to talk, what to think and all men must have a side parting in their hair to be taken seriously. Really, I am not making this stuff up. If anyone told you all this from the beginning, you would never get involved, but of course they don't. It is drip fed, drop by drop, piece by piece. One minute you are floating down this calm stream and before you know it, you have hit the rapids. Some are lucky and bail out when they see it coming, most hang on as they are already committed and then boast about their survival, making them more faithful than those like me, who hang on so tight we nearly drown under the realisation that we were set up in the first place and gasp for breath as we try to prevent anyone else from suffering the same fate. Breakfast over, I decide to venture back through the carpeted maze of the casino to my room and find out what my laptop knows about Emma.

From the privacy of my own space, I google this information (other search engines are available) and with trembling fingers I wait for my computer to explode. Having been taught that any site other than the official site is 'anti' and therefore evil, run by Satan himself, I am extremely wary of the sin of exploring such sites. In fact I am surprisingly terrified. With shaky hands, I figure it is now or never (maybe Elvis' spirit is guiding me) and worth the risk but far from exploding in a dangerous way, to my surprise the laptop explodes only in words, the words that it has held close to its chest for so long, that they come out in a volcanic explosion of rhetoric which overwhelms me. I cannot believe what my eyes are telling me. The Mormon veil is lifted.

CHAPTER 11

My research reaches the point where my worn out brain can take no more and I need to have a distraction. The shock of unexpected words sends me searching for space to collect my thoughts. Someone once said to me that they had never been to Vegas but imagined it to be very claustrophobic to be stuck in a casino, but I guess they found it hard to grasp the vastness of the space. This hotel alone was the largest in the world when it was first built and its numerous outdoor pools, complete with rivers and waterfalls, whirlpools and poolside massage points cover over six acres of relaxation, none of which I will even venture towards on this trip. There are over twenty restaurants that I know of, not to mention the various night clubs and numerous theatres housing anyone from David Copperfield to Cirque de Soleil shows and the main Arena which must hold well over sixteen thousand people, oh, and did I mention the shopping mall, food court and monorail? There may be many problems with Vegas but claustrophobia is not one of them. I am glad for that.

Another beautiful oxymoron about Vegas is that although I feel the desert around me, I can stay here for as long as it takes and never see the outside world unless I choose to. A labyrinth of walkways and corridors lead from one casino to the next and time disappears into the abyss. I wander for a while, perusing the odd gift shop, stopping to investigate the reason for the sporadic cheering at some American Football game and I buy some sunglasses to hide the pain in my eyes.

At one point I do think about visiting the site of the old fort 'those people' occupied on the corner of Las Vegas Boulevard and Washington Street but I see no point, it now has a new history and has its own trip advisor visitors. Even in 1857 the leaders couldn't agree and the fort was abandoned while some of 'those people' went off to fight in the Utah War, defending their stance insisting that they were not ignoring federal law, of course. No, the remains of the sad old fort are not for me, they are evidence of things discarded but I only have to look in the mirror for that. I find a seat in the busy casino allowing me the luxury of resting my body and exercising my mind.

Joseph Smith founded this religion based on an angel visitation and we were taught that throughout his life he was guided by angels and given access to some golden plates, which he translated with the help of prayer and seer stones into scripture, which eventually became the book that haunts me. He was born in Vermont in 1805, but his family moved to western New York by the time he was twelve and this was the area of the 'burned-over' district, a place that was literally saturated with such intense religious revivalism that it was referred to as the Second Awakening. The story was that Joseph was confused over which religion to join so he prayed about it and with the help of angel visitations was told not to join any but instead would be given the tools to re-establish the one and only true church, the original church that ended when Jesus was crucified. The story was told in detail and somehow it made sense, but then if someone tells you something often enough you can start to believe anything.

Vegas is liberated enough to tell me the parts those righteous leaders left out. My thoughts return to the period of my earlier laptop revelations. From the desert depths I have unearthed that Joseph was often accused of 'glass-looking,' claiming to be a treasure seeker, able to find stolen or buried treasure of silver and gold with the help of his seer stones. The lack of any significant successful outcome of his treasure seeking suggests he was simply an imposter and led to court proceedings against him, the results of which remain sketchy. It is with this shocking knowledge that I realise that the beloved Prophet Joseph's character is called into question, but for everything I read, the organisation has an answer: they are all rumours instigated by Satan to discredit this righteous saint. Do I really want to deal with Satan? Joseph is a force for good or evil and there seems to be no middle ground so maybe the key is to find out what happened to Emma after Joseph was killed (martyred of course) in Carthage Jail back in 1844. The expectation is that she would have been devastated, of course, but also there should be a reason why Brigham Young was chosen as the next prophet instead of one of Joseph and Emma's sons and I wonder what that was.

Did Emma herself follow the new Prophet Brigham over the plains, as he continued Joseph's work by leading the pioneers to 'safety' from unhappy mobs to colonise Salt Lake City with her children? The mental neon word, 'NO' startles me. There is no going back. No wonder they don't want you to read this stuff.

A shudder brings me back to my busy surroundings. It is amazing to me that these people around me go about their lives oblivious of the restrictions I have lived by and yet they seem quite happy to be living under Satan's influence. I did not imagine there would be so much happiness and joy etched on their faces when as non members, they are on the slippery road to eternal darkness. We are taught that they knew about the one true church in the pre-existence, the period before birth, but their lack of faith has blinded them to it on earth. That is why missionaries and members like me have a mission to save them, to help them recommit and recall the truths they once knew. It doesn't look like many of them want saving, Vegas seems to be nursing any wounds they have just fine. How I would be judged by 'those people' for sitting here in this den of iniquity, in the company of sinners, surrounded by excess of every kind and not be horrified by the depravity of it all? I could have a drink, but I don't want one, but I also don't want to judge those who do, I am tired of being judged, so the last thing I want to do is judge others. The fact that I feel so at home in this perceived snake pit is an indication of how far I have fallen from grace to some, but I am beginning to realise that there are some really good people out there who don't actually need saving. In fact, the obvious reality is slowly dawning on me, the realisation that of all the people I can see, the one who needs saving most is me.

Eventually, I decide on a trip to Venice, yes, the world is literally at my feet here, from Egypt to Paris I can take a tour around the world without leaving the Strip. A lofty monorail ride later and I arrive at 'The Venetian' who takes me back in time and space via a tribute to the landmarks of Venice. From the romance of the gondola rides along the Grand Canal, to a replica of St Mark's Square providing entertainment from the infamous living statues to various musicians and artistes wandering the cobbled streets to amuse the excited crowds.

An outside gondola ride through the desert sunshine can be extended to a gondola ride through the bustling indoor shopping mall, as you glide effortlessly under the Bridge of Sighs. The sky above is still a dramatic turquoise and the occasional fluffy cloud belies the fact that you are now sailing through a busy casino. Even the sky in Vegas is an artistic illusion and your senses are quickly confused. Intricate hand-painted frescoes replicating original Venetian works of art take you back to the Renaissance period as dawdling tourists idle on the replica Venice bridges to watch the gondolas drift under, often to hear couples being serenaded by the striped jersey wearing, straw-hatted gondoliers. This is not your average shopping mall.

It is a great place to people watch and I intend to do just that. An authentic Italian street side café, offers me a sanctuary for drink and a vantage point from which I can let my imagination tell me the stories of the people passing by. The couples in love, the retirees, the young travellers, the arguments, the making up, the inquisitive children, the other people watchers, the salesmen, the shoppers, the camera shooters, the selfie stick holders. Those who brunch, or lunch or somewhere in between. When you are alone, the world will fool you that everyone else is coupled in bliss, but as we already know, the mind can easily be fooled. My mind drifts back to the words spewing from the intestines of Pandora's box.

Emma didn't follow Brigham Young because they didn't agree on many things and there were several reasons, notably his active polygamy and his involvement in Joseph's polygamy. The one thing that most people know about 'those people', if they know nothing else, is that they are synonymous with polygamy, so no surprise there. Yet, in all my years in this organisation, I was taught (and bear in mind I was teacher myself) that if this question was brought up, we should laugh and say 'polygamy used to be around, but modern day revelation ended it years ago'. End of discussion. At no point were we ever told that Joseph was other than devoted to his only wife Emma. So did Joseph have more than one wife? It seems inconceivable. Anyway, what did she do? Here we have a woman who was happily married to the love of her life, raised and grieved over lost children together, she nursed him through the tarring and feathering that he encountered due to the hostility of mobs set against them, she wrote endearing letters to him in jail, endured all the hardships that his religious claims bombarded their family with and was instrumental (pardon the pun) in creating the hymn book still used today and setting up the organisation for women where her picture still hangs in chapels all over the world, so what did she do to continue Joseph's work? Certainly, in such a patriarchal organisation she was limited, but surely one of her sons would carry on their father's work? I cannot believe the words I read:

Emma and her family left the church.

It left me suddenly standing in quicksand.

CHAPTER 12

My people watching turns inwards as I consider how hard it is to explain what it does to your psyche when your world is turned upside down. Imagine suddenly finding out that two plus two doesn't actually make four, those evil teachers made it all up and by the way the world is square and not round, so you may actually fall off the edge. Maybe then you can imagine the kind of thoughts and feelings currently coursing through my veins. It is reeling, it makes your mind spin like the ball on a roulette wheel and you don't know where you will land or where you want to land. Decades of your life beliefs washed away in a tsunami of truth will leave you clinging to anything, and at the same time afraid to hang on. I need to stop inwardly shaking.

With Aristotle's spirit watching over me, I make a move to regain my composure and take a short walk towards the skeletal celestial globe of the giant golden Armillary Sphere. A stark reminder of the need to mend my sacred hoop. The wise old blackbird who taught me patience builds a circular nest by no random act, Black Elk teaches of the power of the world in unbroken circles.

Soon, I find myself leaving Renaissance Italy and being thrust unceremoniously back into the issues of the modern day as I come face to face with the chance to audition virtually for Simon Cowell or be interviewed by Oprah, as Madame Tussaud's grapples for my attention. I pass on this opportunity and head back to the familiar comforting arms of my hotel room. The words are still scattered on the floor so vividly that I constantly trip over them. Laptop closed. Information unbearable. I collapse back on the bed and fight the urge to disappear under the sheets forever. A few tears of reality, sadness, anger and grief later, my Yorkshire spirit rescues me, another ribbon binds the broken circle and I take a moment to reflect.

Of all the things I hoped to get from this trip, finding out I was right after all had never really occurred to me. I expected to be wrong, they had taught me that I was always wrong, wrong to doubt, wrong to question, wrong earrings, wrong marital status, wrong dress sense, just wrong, everything about me was wrong. Now I find out I am right to doubt, right to question. I am not sure what to do with this information.

I have the language I have been taught. 'Those people' took my words and replaced them with their own. Do not build your testimony on shifting sands. Choose the right. Follow the prophet. Doubt your doubts (before you doubt your faith). Trust your leaders. Dare to do right. Keep the commandments. Stand in holy places. I bear my testimony that this is the one and only true church. I know the church is true. I am a Mormon, I know it, I live it, I love it. These phrases and hundreds more roll off the tongue, I have heard them so many times. Only those who have shared my journey will understand the relevance of popcorn on the apricot tree, the flameless fireside, burning in the bosom, witnessing the sweet spirit, early morning seminary, not breaking the Sabbath, the cultural hall, fast Sunday (which is really slow), free agency, high council, president, stake, ward council and the veiled threat of 'we missed you at church today'. Only now do I realise the extent to which they have invaded my space, my body, my life, my language, they have neutralised my linguistic speaking voice and infiltrated my phraseology. I need to buy a new dictionary. I need to learn to speak again and then I will find my voice. By early evening, I feel the need to drag myself briefly out of my comfort zone to prevent my urge to become a recluse and waste the evening watching mindless reality TV, so I take action.

The coffee shop in The Mirage is busy. Outside, the volcano is erupting and next to me are people waiting to go and see a ventriloquist show. Welcome to Vegas. Tables are fully occupied, but luckily I find a spot hidden in the corner at a rather pleasant table for one. I am slowly drowning in the decadence of a five dollar bottle of water. The Mirage and it is all a mirage. My companion is telling me I can't do this but I am past listening to shallow advice so I study the bottle in silent conversation. The object of this exercise is to be amongst strangers as happy as I can be in my own skin, which is hardly at all. All I can think about is going back to the safety of my own space in my own hotel room but I have set the goal of being out in public for an hour. I need to sit here for at least sixty minutes to get my money's worth from this expensive water, I tell myself in some sort of Yorkshire value for money tradition. I feel consumed by consumerism, which I realise I am enabling. My plastic bottled acquaintance tells me in unspoken words that it is from the islands of Fiji. I feel better, too easily convinced that my five dollars wasn't wasted on Vegas tap water. By the time I learn that it is 'natural artesian water produced by rainfall filtered through volcanic rock over hundreds of years adding vital minerals' (which I feel I need right now), I feel much more at peace with my extravagant purchase. My attention shifts as a young lady in her late twenties asks the couple closest to me if she can share their table and within a few minutes they are swapping their stories. It appears that they are going to the same show.

'Have you seen him before?' she asks the couple.

'No, we haven't, have you?'

'Yes, I saw him a few years ago before he was really famous. He was very good, you will like him. What made you come to this show?' (She omitted the obvious... out of the hundreds of shows in Vegas).

'Oh, we are retired and just wanted to get out of the house for a few days, we don't live too far away and this particular show sounded good.' The husband replies, looking to his wife for approval, which he doesn't need because they are the sort of couple who can speak quite freely for each other and probably finish each others sentences.

'I have just been trekking five days in Death Valley,'

the young lady proudly announces. (I told you there is a five day limit around here). She is keen to tell her story and they are responsive so she continues to describe her experience in this wondrous landscape. 'It was a wonderful experience, the wildlife was amazing, I saw coyotes and bats and lizards.' Her eyes popped like said lizards with the excitement of being able to share her adventure.

'Well that was a very brave thing to do,' the older lady replies admiringly.

I am guessing that the challenging conditions and human limitations in the desert heat create such a beautiful temptress that the fragility of living briefly in unliveable conditions aware of your own mortality is alluring. But what do I know? I am terrified to sit in a coffee shop alone.

'You just have to go with the flow and take it as it comes and then you can deal with anything,' the wise young traveller responds. My ears prick up. I am sensitive to good advice right now and this is a mantra I hear often said in and around Vegas. You can't fight it or you will have a miserable time, you just have to go along with the ride. Maybe that is what I need to remember, I can't fight against the rejection of my former friends as that lies on the road to bitterness, so I should just accept that is the way it is and continue my journey and 'go with the flow'. I make a note of that. Now she is fully on my radar, I am anxiously waiting to hear what other details she has to share about her trip, but to the surprise of both myself and her new friends, she suddenly gets up and announces that the doors will soon be opening for the show and she should to go. She picks up the smallest backpack in the world and vanishes into the night. It seems an abrupt end to their friendship but the wise gentlemen lowers his voice and notes to his wife, 'She is not carrying much baggage, very smart girl.'

I make a note of that too. We all know that too much baggage is a bad thing but to see this traveller wander literally with very little was very effective to witness. I suspect this girl has plenty of baggage but she doesn't carry it around with her. This is the secret. I decide to make a conscious effort to leave my baggage at this coffee shop, not literally of course, I am carrying a small shoulder bag which I will keep with me at all times, I am not crazy.

The man and his wife only have a few seconds of respite before they are joined by a slightly younger but similar couple. They hit it off immediately and appear to have a lot in common. The couple who previously had been engrossed in the young lady's story now let their own life story balloon sail off into the Vegas sky. 'We were just talking with a young girl who has been trekking through Death Valley. Isn't that marvellous? I didn't put my travelling shoes on until I was forty five,' the gentleman reveals. 'There are so many opportunities these days to travel. Our nephew is twenty seven and is free and single so he is currently in France playing for a semi-professional volleyball team, isn't that wonderful?'

I sense this is going to turn into a different type of conversation where various family members are pitted against each other to show how much they have achieved, so I turn my attention to the smartly dressed professional-looking lady who is sitting at the table the other side of me all this time. She has a laptop computer on the table and she has not looked up from it once. Her silent body language conversation screams, 'don't disturb me' and so she has not been interrupted. I guess she is preparing something for an important meeting. She is alone. Maybe like me, she is killing time. Her use of technology makes me look archaic with my notebook but I prefer the feel of pen and paper when writing, it feels like my blood is the ink that writes its story on the page. But I make a mental note that the laptop looks cooler and more business-like. Maybe people think I am writing my shopping list. Suddenly a man enters. A quite distinguished-looking man, tall, well-dressed in a smart suit and he approaches her table. Without a single word, he sits opposite her. She doesn't flinch, stop her concerto fingers or say anything. I am bemused. I think my natural reaction would have been to at least look up, yet he doesn't speak either. Surely he should have asked her if it was okay for him to join her. A few minutes go past and I resign myself to the fact that some things I just don't understand. Then out of nowhere, he speaks to her by leaning over the table and whispering something in her ear. She replies that she is nearly ready. A couple of seconds later, she turns the computer slightly towards me as she switches it off and gathers up her belongings and wanders off with this man, who it now appears she is clearly very familiar with. He suddenly looks like her long-suffering husband. The most shocking thing to me is the fact that there is no important business document being closed down on the computer screen, it is a cartoon type computer game. She has fooled us all. 'This is the 'Mirage', where not everything is what it appears to be', is the final note in my book for today, my hour is up.

The volcano is erupting again as I leave. This time it transfixes me. The display erupts in a fiery orange fountain of yellow flames encompassing the full spectrum of colours in between. Such luminosity spurts unconditional love, sunlight intensified, showing me there is wisdom in my intellectual fight, but also that I should remember to embrace the warrior spirit of the love and learning to be found on this daring search for twilight truth. I am embracing all shades of golden nugget yellow.

CHAPTER 13

It is funny how the brain goes into overdrive at night. Here I am in the most luxurious bed and my mind is having a party and not a happy one, more like a drunken, depressed and somewhat maudlin one, and remember I don't drink.

'Those people' once told me that my illness, the presence of my silent companion is due to the fact that I sinned before I was born. I believed them. It did seem like a punishment. My journey for truth is turning towards myself, learning not to punish myself for the lies they taught me, which multiplied my inbred fears. One truth is that they have destroyed me, but another is that I let them. Hating myself came easy and they confirmed I was a sinner for not being perfect. If things are to change for the better, I need to believe in myself, trust myself and move forward. Sounds like a lot of easy cliches but with all due respect to Lionel Richie it feels like dancing on the ceiling, a nice idea but potentially impossible and definitely dangerous. But, if Interstate 15 knows my name then maybe it is the long road home.

My heart has belonged to America since my first glimpse of the naughty glint in Gene Kelly's eye coming through my parents black and white TV and my first visit thirty years ago sealed that love. That was when I was first introduced to my Native American name and only now am I beginning to understand it. I am grateful to those who allowed an outsider like me to be included. That wonderful Teton adventure where I met the man of my dreams only to lose him again shortly after, but at least we had our moment and that was precious.

Deep down everyone just wants love and acceptance. It seems simple, yet we complicate it by dishonouring our differences rather than celebrating them. Vegas likes different. I like Vegas. The irony of displacement is not lost on me. Here, of all the places in the world, nothing is as it seems, holder and embracer of secrets not to be easily revealed. Yet it is here that I can learn my truth. There is space to examine my personal landscape and go to the one place that terrifies me, my own reality. Some would say I could have locked myself in my own home and figured that out, but the pain is so deep, so intensely painful that the only place I could face up to it is in the loving arms of my desert friend who soothes my wounds with the calming balm of time and space. 'Those people' raped my mind and soul, my nemesis raped my body and the destruction is complete. You do not wake up and recover from that in your own bed overnight.

Days after my dad's death, I came face to face with the devil. I was struggling with the burden of not only overcoming the emotional consequences of my dad's death but I had to face and deal with the practicalities. One day I summoned up enormous strength and courage to travel the twenty minutes into the nearest town, find the ever elusive parking space, and face the reality of donating some of my father's possessions to the local charity shop. I told my heavy heart plodding steps that it would be therapeutic to do this, after all it was only stuff, but of course I wasn't easily convinced. It actually felt like I was giving away pieces of my dad's life and with it pieces of my heart. Logic and reason had to prevail, they were no longer useful to us and even if I had room to store them, it would be dead space, someone else could benefit. Old paperbacks that lay unread on his bookshelf, in the hope that one day they would find a cure for the macular degeneration that robbed him of his love of reading. Dusty vinyl records that once played songs which echoed around the house, but which in his final few deaf years deserted him when their sounds were left only to his imagination. The retirement clock that marked the passage of not only his career but his time on earth and which stopped shortly after he did, batteries exhausted and finally extinguished. Worn clothes that could still house another which hung expectantly in the wardrobe waiting in vain for their owners' return, they needed to be set free to walk the streets again. My heart wouldn't break today, it would strengthen, I told myself. My dad was not the stuff and he would want them to go to help others and so fighting the urge to cling on forever, I passed them on and left the shop stifling any embarrassing tears. I had done it. My return journey to the car park was physically lighter but emotionally tender with an acceptance that however different it may be, life does go on. Then I turned the corner and came face to face in a meeting that was unavoidable, with a church leader who had for many years been my confidante, my mentor, my friend. He smiled, so I smiled back. I am nothing if not congenial, but my naivety blinded me from the smiling assassin. We greeted each other like the long lost friends we once were, exchanging pleasantries and then he brought up the church.

'They need a new bishop, the old one is moving away.'

The thought crossed my mind that he was angling for the job himself and while my mind was distracted, my mouth went on ahead. 'That's good,' I quipped. I only met the old bishop once. He was walking from his car into the chapel with his scarf swung around his neck like a 1950s college professor. I remember because he pushed passed me to get through the door first, ignoring me in the process and I made a mental note that he was one to watch.

'Don't be like that,' the devil chastised as if I was a naughty school girl. I felt suitably rebuked. He now had the upper hand and he knew it. In a desperate need to deflect the trajectory of the conversation, I panicked and suddenly words were pouring from my mouth before I could prevent them. I asked how the recent same sex marriage laws had affected him as a counsellor of wisdom. Red rag. Bull. He saw the red. I touched a nerve. His eyes pierced me like sharpened javelins. 'Wow, you really have lost your testimony,' he declared, looking at me like the leper he thought I was. I was totally taken aback. Until then, however stupid it may seem, I had never considered I had lost anything of worth in that way, but only gained knowledge.

'Testimony of the gospel or of the church?' Where that question came from I don't know but I was on the back foot.

'The Church.'

I breathed a sigh of relief and also the realisation dawned on me for the first time that 'those people' bear testimony of the church, not the Gospel. Talk about the penny dropping, it fell like a two pound coin. I never realised the two were separated and now there was no church for me. It suddenly made sense and I instantly felt nauseous. In an effort to calm the situation and change the subject, I blurted out that my dad had just passed away. I guess I thought he would be compassionate. But there was silence. I continued, unusually for me, finding the silence uncomfortable, 'well at least we can agree to disagree, we all end up in the same place anyway.' I gave him a 'get out' so we could shake hands and walk away. But no. His fiery eyes bore into my soul.

'Are you sure?' he responded with venom. 'I don't think you and your family are going the same place as mine. You have given your future away by the decisions you have made. Your future is unclear and your dad's present is unclear. Who knows where he is.' Basically his words punched me in the face. I can't even recall how I responded but I walked away so he didn't see the tears that I had tried all day to stifle. Ultimately, he did me a huge favour. What 'Christian' person in their right mind would react in such a way? There was no compassion, religious or moral. Unwittingly, he confirmed that I had not actually lost anything and their gospel testimony is distorted. I had to tend to my invisible wounds. That conversation helped me to decide that no longer would I allow them to tell me what I had or what I was, I had to find my own power. He no longer held my respect, I saw some true colours for the first time and if I have ever seen evil personified it was in that moment.

My tortured mind continues to exercise throughout the night until eventually the darkness eats my thoughts and exhaustion sends me a couple of hours of relief in dark restless sleep.

Eventually, after time in a distant place, the morning light wakes my tired body to the realisation that I have nothing to say today. The words and the page are not speaking and I feel deflated. Is it a hopeless cause? Is my voice carried away on the wind and above the ears of all around me? Doubt is a contagious disease and self doubt will hurtle you towards depression and inactivity before you have time to blink, so I force myself into action and prepare to at the very least shower and dress and show the world that I am there.

An hour or so later I am ready but not sure what for. The annoying inner voice seems to think I should be busy doing something but the reality is that I am tired, very tired, and maybe the world is not for me today. My brain is overloaded, I need to take a breather and collect my thoughts. I will be kind to myself today, relax and see what happens, because right now I have nothing left but despair.

CHAPTER 14

I am not very good at relaxing. It is a foreign language to me, but my hotel has a spa. I am not very good at being around other ladies in various stages of nakedness and beauty routines in general. I don't even wear make up unless I really have to, so I look for the least invasive treatment. A manicure. I can do that. I head down to the spa before I can change my mind. I have never been to a spa before, so now I feel like a dehydrated fish. I am greeted by a professional but fairly dull receptionist who points me in the direction of the waiting area and tells me that Marie will be with me in about ten minutes. I head down the stairs and pass another reception desk where a well manicured lady asks if I will require a robe. I hope I didn't recoil in horror, but I know I probably did. I simply don't feel comfortable in these surroundings to start with and I want to stay fully dressed at all times and then my head starts playing games. Why would I need a robe for a manicure? I shake off the doubts, realising that I am at the point of no return and I am ushered into the waiting area. It is a fern-filled space with white reclining chairs and comfortable sofas. A lady dressed in a robe with no inhibitions is reclining with some form of face pack on her face. It feels as if I am interrupting something so I walk around a screen, find a deserted sofa relaxing against the wall and introduce myself to it. I feel conspicuous. Looking around, I see a table with fresh fruit and water machines. The thought crosses my mind that I could take a complimentary piece of fruit but I decide against it in my fear that Marie turns up and I end up trying to act casual with a half eaten apple and subsequent juice all over my fingers. I decide to get some water. It is a spa, so of course the water is made with slices of water melon floating on the top like delicate synchronised swimmers and tastes delicious. I finish three cups before Marie turns up, so I could have eaten the apple.

Marie is a larger than life character full of personality. She is very forceful in her directions and, to be honest, a bit intimidating. My doubting and panic reach crescendo level, but it is too late I am committed. Remembering the advice from last night, I decide to embrace the experience and go with it. The process starts with a scrub being massaged on my hands and arms up to my elbows, yes, I admit the robe would have been a good idea, but how was I to know? It is all wonderfully relaxing, I will admit. Then I am guided to a seat opposite Marie, as she very expertly goes about her business. She knows what she is doing, which is good as I have no idea. She is also extremely good at testing if you want to talk or how much she can open up to you. At first with me she is a little guarded. I can understand that, I am still doing my flailing fish impression and my anxiety I imagine by now is painted as a deep blush on my face.

'What colour do you want on your nails?' Marie asks as though it is the easiest question in the world. I think she is also using it as an ice breaker to cool my flushing brow. I am embarrassed to admit I have no clue. I am a virgin at this manicure thing. What is colour anyway?

'Maybe just clear, my nails are not that good,' I blurt out in embarrassed tones.

'My dear, let me explain, the worse you feel about your nails or anything else, then disguise it with colour. You need a bit of colour in your life, leave it to me.'

That is it. The most profound statement I have heard so far. This lady is someone I need to be in the moment with. So I leave it to her. She tries a few colours which all look the same to me but settles on 'blushing pink peach' which reminds me of the bowl of complimentary fruit and although at some level an oxymoron, it turns out that it is just perfect for me, so I know I am literally in good hands.

'So where are you from?' She senses I need a distraction from my fear.

'England.'

'Ah! Cups of tea and cucumber sandwiches with the Queen,' she mocks me in her fake English accent. 'Have you ever met the Queen?'

I decide to be honest. I am in Vegas, I can be myself today. 'To be honest, I don't really care for the Royal Family.' There I put it out there and wait for a response. It takes longer than I thought, so I add, 'I liked Diana.' That phrase releases a trust between us that is now free to fly.

'Oh we loved Diana.' She moves her head closer to mine and holds my hand more firmly, 'Tell me, do you think they killed her?'

Okay. I wasn't expecting that but at this point I have nothing to lose. 'Yes, I do.' Gulp.

'Oh so do I.'

Thank goodness. I appear to have said the right thing and this unleashes a whole discussion about the circumstances of Diana's death, the possibilities if she had lived, the horror of Charles and Camilla and all hope now on William and Kate. Marie is now wound up and ready to go. 'It is shocking how Charles used her and don't get me started on Camilla. I am from New York and if any woman had done that in my family she would be taken into the bathroom for a chat by my sisters and she wouldn't be leaving in the same way, if you know what I mean.' She laughs in her big booming voice. 'We don't take too kindly to messing with us like that, we've got each other's backs.' I like her even more. I want to be her sister so bad that I begin to open up myself.

'I met Diana once. Well I didn't meet her but I saw her. She was unveiling some plaque and I was about fifty yards away. I know it sounds ridiculous but she had such an aura, she was like a bright light shining in the crowd, she was just someone you wanted to be around,' I confided. It was a concern that I had said too much, but she considered my statement and I saw in her eyes that we had connected.

'I know what you mean. One of my sisters saw Nelson Mandela and she said the same thing about him and Mother Theresa, of course, she had it. Now I don't know if you believe in God but it is some kind of spiritual light.' I told her I did believe in God and I thought she was right. She had more spirituality around her than I had witnessed for a long time.

My nails are nearly finished, they look amazing but I want her to keep going. I don't want it to end. I could stay here talking to her all day. I am so sad that my treatment is over and at the prospect of leaving, but as that moment dawns on my face, she pulls me close and whispers, 'I have been doing this for twenty five years and I have worked with some of the most famous people, but I never tell because that is their business, but I know the good ones. You are one of the good, genuine ones. Don't ever change.'

There are so many words I want to say to her but they are enclosed in tear-filled eyes. I feel as though I am leaving my best friend and I have only known this woman for a few minutes. How does that work? Before I have chance to cling to my new friend and never let her go, she is gone and I felt better for having met her, which is the biggest compliment I can give. I remember the old man back home crossing the road, this is what he was teaching me too. If you hear the same message twice from different people, you need to listen. When you strip all the egos, dogma and drama away, making people feel better for having been in your presence, isn't that real life? There it is.

My brief encounter with Marie presented me with a fleeting moment of friendship and a lifetime of learning and her insightful joie de vive gave me pinks of every shade. At first I began noticing the numerous tones of pink on long fingernails, but before long I was taking photographs of pinks of all tones in all directions. The hint of salmon pink in the evening desert sky, rosy pink t-shirts, sweets, ice creams, and cakes. Shocking hot pink lights on the giant neon signs, posters and street signs and the steel pink wig of the drag queen on the strip. The flamingo pink sequinned dress of the fake Vegas show girl, posing for photos for dollars and the watery orange pink reflections in the Bellagio fountains.

Everyone is trying to stand out and assert their own identity by trying desperately to fit in and blend into the emotional landscape. Marie has shifted my consciousness. I listened to 'those people' and in the process sacrificed myself and everything I stood for. They manipulated my vulnerability, but I betrayed myself. One day I would love to find her again, to thank her.

CHAPTER 15

I hit the slot machines. Now when I say, 'I hit the slot machines', I mean I sidled up to them in a very conspicuous way and casually slid sideways on to one of the seats looking around to see if anyone was watching. I could not have looked more suspicious if I had been wearing a Columbo coat and dark glasses, so I wonder if my hidden security team are still watching me. If so, was it because I looked like a devious black book potential or did I look like an old dear who didn't know what she was doing?

Anyway, here I am, waiting once again to be zapped for sinful behaviour and misdemeanour. It doesn't happen immediately, so I examine the machine for instructions. There aren't any. There really should be, I thought to myself, otherwise how do all these other people know what to do? Dispersed throughout this vast space are various other people playing these talkative machines but they all look like they know what they are doing. Some of them are older than me, preciously guarding cups full of coins. They are clearly here for the day. In a way I kind of admire their commitment and make a mental note to open a care home that is like a casino, bright lights, noise, lots of distractions and one armed bandits for people to play mindlessly to help occupy their time (all machines taking tiddlywinks instead of money of course), I think I may be on to something.

Realising my lack of strength, my own one armed bandit needs two arms to pull down the handle. Closing my eyes, which apparently is not the way most gamblers roll in Vegas (but I don't think I am a born to be high roller) I miss the visual thrill of the uncertain outcome. The closing of the eyes is only effective in having the joy of opening them to see that Satan has still not arrived in person, but I miss seeing the lovely fruits spin to a non-conformist stop, indicating that I have lost my money. Excited to try again, this time I keep my eyes open. However, before you think I have lost all my integrity, I have only lost one dollar at this point and so have four more to go. These four dollars last me several entertaining minutes and I have to confess I enjoy my first illicit affair with this machine. It doesn't reward me for my bravery but it teaches me many things. First of all, there is a button you can press so you don't have to pull the handle (genius). Secondly, it probably helps to read some instructions online first so that at least you know what the spin button does, although apparently it is not too relevant to the outcome. Third and most important, playing the slots is like just having toast every morning when you could go as far as a daily full English breakfast: the tables are where you need to be for the full experience but that is a step too far for me right now.

The point of the slots is that loners like me can avoid social contact and for a beginner that is all I need today.

Don't get me wrong, I am not advocating gambling, but if you have self control (which to be honest is something I have too much of) and you can stick to an affordable budget, it is a pleasant way to spend a few hours once in a lifetime. Vegas will not get rich on this Yorkshire girl. However, much to my surprise I am enjoying myself, which isn't supposed to happen. I suddenly feel a small twinge of liberation and I like it. No wins, but a sneaky Krispy Creme donut to take back to my room finds me surprisingly content. Don't judge me.

The laptop calls me back to work. So if Emma left the organisation, I am on the right path, even if totally unexpected. Walking on unstable ground is never easy but this gives a whole new meaning to 'shifting sands'. I have to steady myself to remember which is the floor and which is the ceiling as the information in front of me rocks the foundation of my beliefs. My next revelation concerns the Book of Mormon itself. It is a dull read but we are taught it is sacred scripture from beginning to end, from introduction to index, it is all supposed to be prophetic and inspirational. This is the North Star of consistency, the gospel never changes, only people do, the phrases I have been indoctrinated with run off my tongue with alarming ease even today. Then from the shadows the electronic screen suddenly shouts at me. The unchangeable book has been changed. It was never publicly announced, explained, elaborated, but was pushed in through the back door in the dead of night in a simple publishing rewrite. It is one word. I had no idea, but I check it out with the book burning a hole in the chair next to me and it is true. One word, but it rewrites history.

Previously they taught that Native Americans are direct descendants of the Lamanites (Nephi being the hero of the book and Laman being his naughty brother) but there is no factual evidence of this and modern DNA studies do not support it. Aware of this development in DNA studies, an amendment was made in 2006. Originally the book stated: 'After thousands of years, all were destroyed except the Lamanites, and they are the principal ancestors of the American Indians.' It now says: 'After thousands of years, all were destroyed except the Lamanites, and they are **among** the ancestors of the American Indians.' Now I personally struggled with the theory that Lamanites were Native Americans anyway, it made no sense, but I suffered quite unwittingly from blind obedience. However, this alteration suggests a certain edging your bets in case of further damning DNA proof being unearthed. From an official prospective and maybe to the lay person, it is a minor discrepancy and basically says the same thing but putting it into context, it potentially changes history and certainly changes the history of the indigenous people, which is a huge deal. Imagine if your whole DNA history was called into question. The real deal breaker is that this is scripture, changed without revelation, but no doubt by now, the introduction is taught in Sunday School as just an introduction and no longer scripture, the tides turn so fast. The sad reality is that they reckon that it is only my generation that has to be phased out before all these 'new truths' will be gospel to the next generation and all incongruities will be forgotten and then history will repeat itself with the next generation and so on. Like Chinese whispers, it never ends but distorts. Ironically 'those people' will say it was announced out there on the internet, the same internet that we were all warned not to explore.

I have heard enough to know that I have been duped. It makes me sick to my stomach and the words continue to rain like bullets from the screen as it continues to unearth the hundreds of recent changes to the scriptures, claiming them to be merely in the main grammatical corrections, or correcting minor typographical errors but at the same time altering historical references and proving at the very least that for so called 'prophets', the book was clearly poorly produced the first time. I also discover that it is much harder to find details of the changes on the official website (although they are there if you have the patience to look) than to learn how to buy the new version of the scriptures, which are graded from 'economy' to 'simulated leather' and a new 'upgraded genuine leather,' all very relevant, as any self-respecting member would have to own a copy of these new scriptures (at of course their own expense). But I am sure no one at church would judge the economy scripture holder. Right? Quite a hugely successful business deal if all fifteen million members buy them, which they will, or risk being judged accordingly.

The more I discover, the more it feels like a corporation, a business venture, a shady pyramid scheme. These 'men of God' appear to be protecting their financial assets more than being shepherds watching over their flock. Maybe there is more to this financial side of the history. If you seek, you will find. Another surprise lies in wait.

Unbelievably, I discover that the church sneakily resurrected the Perpetual Emigration Fund, ushering it furtively in through the back door in 2001, renaming it as the Perpetual Education Fund and rebranding it as a form of positive self-reliance. The programme is funded through contributions of Church members and others who support its mission. It is a revolving resource in which money is loaned to an individual to help pay for training or advanced education. When a student has graduated and is working, he or she then pays back the loan at a low interest rate. Repayments allow for future loans. In other words, members pay for this fund, members in need benefit from it, but pay it back with interest and that goes back into the fund to help others. I remember thinking that was a great idea at the time, unaware of its history, but now I see the genius of making the church a healthy profit whilst at the same time the members pay for it. The financial records are a closed and sealed book, so combine the PEF with the compulsory ten percent tithe every member is forced to pay and the significant income from special clothing for the temple, secret underwear for every member, books and study materials, art and music specially produced for church members, travel to various church events, the list goes on and the church gets richer. It is still running today but to benefit from it you need to be:

- *A temple-worthy member of The Church of Jesus Christ of Latter-day Saints.*
- *18 years of age or older.*
- *If a young single adult, be enrolled and active in an institute of religion (married students and those over 30 are not required to attend institute).*
- *Live and attend school in a PEF-approved country. Currently, PEF is not available in the United States or Canada.*

So the church will help you, but only if the church owns you and suddenly we are back in the 1800s.

The light has faded. After dark, the lights of Vegas sing their oratorio to the desert sky. This is where we can bear witness to the brightest and the best in camouflage. The midnight screams look at my beauty, look at the fun I am having, whilst all the time deflecting your eyes away from the broken people and from where they run.

'Those people' judge this scene in a righteously moral way and do not understand that one bad call can take it all away, and it may not be your doing but it will certainly be your ruin. A divorce, an illness, a redundancy, a death, a debt, a starving child or living with an abusive mind, a repossession, a dispossession, an indiscretion, a tattooed stain on the hand that feeds into a whirlwind of downward destruction leads to life outside 'those people' and their expectations. Bad luck = Sin. Repent or die. Heaven or Hell.

All of these and more will bind you to a reality that was never on the cards but it is the hand you were dealt and only here where the cards are redealt, if but for a fleeting moment, there is escape and sometimes hope washed down with desperation and perspiration, sweating on a roll of the dice or a spin of the wheel and somewhere in-between and deep down we just don't know how to feel. Lady luck prostitutes herself on the last throw and once again the doors close.

Meanwhile the desert silently calls your name but no one hears. The answers lie in-between the particles of dust out under the starry night sky, more answers than questions but no one is looking. The dried bones of those who came before are hidden in secret of wrongs righted and evil personified, but the desert will give up her secrets. 'Those people' won't. The pain they have caused me is so indescribable, it is like trying to mark the sorrow at Wounded Knee.

To some, I am like silence, to be avoided at all cost, the space between the words is offensive to them as it scares them so much. It must be obliterated, they cannot stand its honesty. Silence is forced to make a suicidal swim for the shore, but sinks amid the smothering sounds. For me, silence is precious. Silence is silver.

CHAPTER 16

My hotel room is a safe refuge from the storm of life. I have only borrowed it for a short time and so it reflects a different energy back at me as a comfortable friendly stranger. I am just a visitor passing through and as such any burden of responsibility is lifted from my aching shoulders. My dripping tap is not a nightmare of internet searching for reliable plumbers (or slightly unreliable as long as they are not psychopaths) but a phone call to reception and ten minutes later it is fixed and suddenly by way of compensation for being a responsible, yet undemanding guest, apparently, I am indulging in a luxurious complimentary fruit platter.

From my vantage point on the window sill, which still makes for a comfy seat, I hug my knees, turning my face once again to the large window, to press my cheek against the glass. The train of New York-New York is riding through the sky, glass houses throwing and catching stones in every direction and the invisible lions roar. Many years ago the lions were here, I saw them as they watched through their misted eyes, the people locked in their human cage. Now at last they can roam invisibly free and protect their ground.

Contrails fleetingly dance to the music of their travellers, conversing a brief story of hopes and dreams ending or beginning. Minutes later, the cornflower blue sky speaks differently when there are no clouds or contrails to interrupt his conversation. Father Sky seductively dances above Mother Earth looking after her needs, watering her fertile soil, caressing her with his gentle breeze. There is no doubt he loves her, if only we did too.

I guess there is no hiding place here and the truth comes out eventually. 'Those people' who hide in their clouds will not stay long before they are exposed. I say 'those people' but a lot of them are innocent victims. I should know, I was one of them at one time, but I am also embarrassed and devastated to know that many actually know the truth but turn a blind eye for various reasons. Perhaps it would mean too much change for them to handle. They could seriously break apart their family, they would have to confront wasting so many years on a falsehood, being deceived, possibly lose their job, their scholarship, their home, their marriage, their family, the list goes on and I know someone in each of those scenarios, but saddest is that people do not like to change and stepping out of the familiar space into unfamiliar is paralysing to some. Fear of the unknown ironically keeps them in bondage by the untrue, deceitful, dishonest nature of the corporation.

When did I change from the girl with the dreams in her eyes to the ghost I became? Maybe it was just the perfect storm, my invisible companion, the fear, 'those people' predators looking for the innocent and vulnerable all just converging at the wrong or right time and I was sucked under a tsunami of belief that my childish reflection was lying and I would never fulfil those innocent dreams. I should have believed in myself and in the truth of the original road map in my eyes. Too bad it has taken so long for me to realise.

'Those people' tend to gravitate to young, impressionable, isolated lost souls and offer a family bond, a kinship, a safe harbour in the storm, but all the time they control the wind that manages the waves, and I, like many others, are blissfully led astray, expecting to learn how to walk on water but instead being held down to drown beneath the waves.

I hate the person they made me, they destroyed the little confidence I had. They emphasised all my family's inherited fears and I had no idea that with some self-esteem I could have prevented it, but that's how they were able to manipulate. However, despite all the obstacles, I am loving the person I am very slowly becoming. My sad house is starting to smile again. There is a reason why mountains are symbolic of prayer, spirituality or whatever makes you comfortable: the view from the top is an accomplishment and far more satisfying if you have lived in the valley, but it is one hell of a climb. Their book is suddenly of no importance. My world is becoming more colourful, the grey streets are lightening their grip on the souls of my shoes. I can walk barefoot.

The raven blends in with the branches. Only when the coloured ribbons blow do you see the pain. The road you walk is the unwritten story of your silent footsteps.

It is your road and yours alone. No one else will walk this path, you are unique. Make it a road to somewhere.

**This caged bird is now free to fly
and she will sing like a canary.**

CHAPTER 17

Feeling like some of the blinkers have been removed, I enjoy today by people watching and exploring the connecting routes between casinos. I invest a few dollars in a young man who is selling his story in the form of a CD, by accosting tourists like myself, but I feel an empathy for him. He tells me that along with his band members he has made the drastic move from New York to Vegas in a final attempt to make it in the music industry, much to the despair of his parents who had expected so much more from him. If this attempt doesn't work, he has promised them he will go home, give up on his dream and 'fit in' with their expectations. I hope he never gives in and I really do hope he isn't making all this up. His eyes tell me he is being honest so I do my bit to help him along, after all, let's face it I have been duped in worse ways than this, and this has only cost me ten dollars rather than ten percent of my entire life earnings, so either way it is a bargain.

I plan to spend some time at the Bellagio, where I can watch the world go by while I wait for the next display of the choreographed musical dancing water fountains to mesmerise my senses. Outside the entrance to the hotel is a large semicircular area especially for visitors to idle away their time, whilst the unseen but obvious anticipation of the next performance dangles over the crowds like a ticket to Disneyland. I love this place, every thirty minutes it transcends reality and transforms the ugliness of the Strip into a ballet of the mind. Thousands of cleverly orchestrated fountains perform across a vast area, arising slowly out of the whimsical mists of hopefulness, surprising their audience with impeccably timed rhythm and movement to music by anything from Broadway classics to operatic greats, every time they move me to tears as they reach a poetic crescendo that showers nearly 550 feet into the heights of possibility. It is romantic, it is sexy, it is transcendent and it is not to be missed. Often a spontaneous round of applause is the only method of appreciation available to the crowds, as for those few minutes they are transported into another world and for that brief moment the people are united by the awakening of the senses. It is a beautiful thing. My re-baptism is complete. I feel like ballet dancing in the fountains.

Tearing myself away, I venture into the hotel's lobby to admire the amazing colourful glass sculptured blossoms that hover like butterflies from the ceiling, Chihuly's 'Fiori Di Como'. It is not the kind of art that you can gaze at quickly and walk past, it captivates and entraps. Finding a vacant seat where I can sit and take in the majesty of this phenomenon, I study the beauty above me and estimate there must be over 2000 square feet. It must be a nightmare to clean. People pass by and comment to their companions, some look up for a few minutes, some like me are taking their time to admire, a small group of students find a spot to lie down to gain a better perspective. This is public art at its best. Like the fountains, it engages people and unites us if but for a few fleeting moments. In that small time and space there is hope for humanity. It is an opportunity to bathe in the primary colours that with renewed vision stand bold in my eyes, and I don't think I have ever been happier.

The seat next to me is occupied by a young man who introduces himself as Chris. He is taking photographs of the artistic ceiling from our shared vantage point. I am intrigued if not still socially awkward but I endeavour to engage in conversation about our shared appreciation of the ceiling. He tells me he is not really a great photographer but is simply captivated by the art work above our heads. We exchange pleasantries and I learn he is visiting from Alaska where he is at university studying Eastern philosophy. Struggling for the right words to say about myself, I tell him I am on my own personal philosophical quest and I am very pleased to have crossed paths with him. I expect that to be the end of our brief conversation and I silently prepare my body to consider moving on to the next location. Chris has other plans.

'Do you need any help?' he volunteers as he notices I am preparing to get up.

'No, thank you, I am fine, just reminding my old body how to move.' I cringe to myself as I realise I must stop saying I am old, my skeletal body is simply older than it should be because of the weightiness of my silent companion but I must remove all my labels not just the religious ones.

'Have you heard of Kintsugi?' His comment intrigues me and I hesitate before trying to move again.

'A Japanese… art?'

'It is much more than that, it is a Japanese technique of mending, kind of a golden joinery, taking for example a broken ceramic pot and repairing it with a special lacquer mixed with gold powder. The philosophy behind it is to incorporate the repair to make it part of the whole. That way the repair is not disguised but actually can make it more beautiful than the original.' He has my attention.

'That's amazing, I had no idea.'

'So if this glass sculpture breaks, it can be repaired in an obvious way and we can celebrate the join, as long as it doesn't land on our heads, of course.' His smile is as bright as his humour. With that he leaps to his feet and holds his hand out to help me up. 'My mom has rheumatoid arthritis, I recognise the unrecognisable, the pain that others don't see. Kintsugi, embrace your wounds.' He smiles a cheeky grin and walks away.

As I make my way through the casino, his words spiral around my brain. There is a silver-haired pianist playing a tune I recognise but have no name for. I pause to appreciate his talent and let my mind wander in the melody. The scars from numerous joint replacements are part of who I am now but nothing prepared me for the horror of the first gruesome sight. Time heals, literally in the physical sense but the landscape of the body is never the same and maybe I have never taken the time to acknowledge that. Kintsugi. Straight after the operations, my own body repulsed me. I was not prepared for the gruesome sight of my own wounded flesh. Months later I settled on that was how it was now and I saw myself as deformed, even ugly and 'those people' confirm that this is proof of my sinful pre-existence. Bastards. There, I said it (oh yes, we were not allowed to swear either so I am working on that too). This is actually the first time I realise these wounds are a physical manifestation of the emotional wounds 'those people' stabbed me with. They are my survival medals, my battle scars which I can now wholeheartedly embrace because I damn well earned these badges, and I must consider them my trophies of my resilience. Quite a mind shift. I am secretly pleased with myself. I am a brave warrior after all. Thank goodness I am in close proximity to the world's largest chocolate factory, I deserve a treat.

A delicious moment and an indulgent tour of an Ansel Adams exhibition later, I make my way back through the casino. The distinguished pianist is still performing in the nearby bar area. He looks as though he has done this for many years, it is so natural to him. Some of his audience are listening even if it is only with their tapping feet, others are oblivious, drowning in their own conversations and literally staring into their glass futures. I wonder how that feels to the professional pianist. Does he care that not all hear his voice? Does he believe that all of them hear something even if they don't know it? More questions I will probably never know the answers to. I contemplate waiting for him to end his set so that I can ask him, but he goes effortlessly from one classical art painting to another and so I leave him alone, and simply relax and escape into his musicality.

The first place any faithful member heads for wherever they are is the temple. There is one here, off the Strip, on the humbly named Temple View Drive, built in decadent sugar white beauty in a prominent place where it can be elevated as a hierarchal heavenly token. Placement of such symbols is a tried and tested psychology, the Statue of Liberty is not positioned at the entrance to the New York Harbor by coincidence, but make no mistake, you would be closer to any god at the top of a literal mountain rather than this temple facsimile. A golden angel adorns one of its icicle steeples, turning his back on the shenanigans of the city as he waits to herald in the Lord's return.

Ironically, there is no enlightenment in this gloriously illuminated building, which attracts moths like any light bulb, but regardless is held in esteem as a symbolic lighthouse calling the sinners home. When I was first allowed inside a temple, I had no idea what to expect. I was told it would be the most spiritual experience ever, because inside everyone is equal, but it was so weird it terrified me. Even then you couldn't ask questions, if you did you simply were not faithful or spiritual enough to understand the symbolism and you were looked down upon accordingly.

Everyone is dressed in special white temple clothes, the idea being that the most prominent members and the least prominent are exactly the same and so this is where Jesus is most likely to hang out. The reality was horrifyingly different. To start with, you have to be an adult member for at least a year (although the rules change constantly so that might have changed by now) and then you have an interview with church officials who tell you they have the power of discernment and can therefore tell if you lie to them. A scary concept even for the brutally honest amongst us, like me. You are asked a number of questions from a script which you are required to answer correctly, to confirm that you obey the sacred covenants you entered into at baptism and that you subsequently promise to attend church, sustain leaders, follow their teachings, and so on, re-enforcing your total and complete commitment. You must specifically acknowledge that Joseph is a true Prophet, and most importantly, pay a full tithe. If you give all the appropriate answers and the leader who is interviewing you has not had any doubts about you, by connecting with his special powers, a slip of paper called a 'recommend', which allows you to enter the temple, is issued. Once inside the temple I found that everyone does indeed wear special temple clothes, white dresses for the women and white suits for the men, but that does not make them in any way equal. Some people have their own individually designed temple wear, often made from wedding dresses and suits, others like me line up to rent a basic plain white gown for the day so the differences are amplified and yes, money does change hands in this temple, so I am not surprised that I never saw Jesus.

The Temple is a place of counterfeit masonic rituals that at best are weird and at worst deceptive. This is also the place you get married, not until death do you part, but for eternity. However, if you don't have that slip of paper you can't enter the temple, so don't expect to go to family weddings, including those of your children unless you are willing to comply. This alone is one reason why some people find it hard to leave, imagine being a parent to six children and not being able to go to any of their weddings. On this there is no compromise, no compassion, and in my opinion, no discernment. Luckily, for me, I first attended the temple after 1990, I say luckily, but maybe that was the unluckiest part because if I had attended sooner, I would have witnessed the red flag that I hope would have stopped me in my tracks, but we will never know now.

Prior to 1990, part of the temple endowment ceremony was to swear a blood oath, in the form of a symbolic gesture of slitting your throat, which I was told later was an indication of your penalty if you told anyone what goes on in the temple. Leaders now say it was referring to if you tell anyone about your pledge with God, not sure it makes a difference, it is still shockingly offensive to me. Obviously, after 1990, God must have thought so too, so it was removed and when I attended I didn't have any knowledge of it.

Everything related to the temple is ornate, from the

manicured, landscaped grounds to the interior elaborate decorations. From Liberace chandeliers to floor to ceiling windows, everything screams of silent decadence, symbolic of the Celestial Kingdom, the highest place in the heavens that we are urged to aim for. If you fall enough from grace to go to one of the lesser two levels, you do not have the all access backstage pass you get at the top and therefore will be separated from faithful family members, who will have to remain in the audience, watching what could have been.

The other big reason to attend the temple is to be baptised vicariously for the dead. This is an activity that particularly children aged twelve and over are actively encouraged to be involved with. They are not allowed a full access pass to the temple, just the baptismal font which is usually in the basement but they will be subject to the same worthiness interview. The names eligible for baptism are created from the intensive family history research that members are expected to perform in detail, which rather than being an opportunity to find out about your own DNA and historical roots, is simply an exercise in keeping busy in this addictive activity which keeps you out of the real world. Children are given lists of names of these unfortunate people who died before they accepted the church (I always thought it was the gospel…..but the lines are now blurry) and they are dunked via full body immersion into the cold water of baptism in an attempt to let the deceased person accept the baptism on the other side of the veil. They are encouraged to do as many as possible one after another, so one person can be dunked several times in a row for various strangers. Rumours that Hitler has been vicariously baptised always run riot, but who knows, anything is possible. A few years ago the church had to apologise for an 'individual' member submitting the names of Jewish Holocaust victims for posthumous baptism. Says it all really.

There is a big emphasis on mirrors, which are placed strategically so that your image is reflected back at you a hundred times, in a symbolic representation that your soul lives forever, in the eternities. This impressed me immensely until one day, many years later it was pointed out to me that in most rooms you can create this effect if you place mirrors in different rooms pointed in the right direction. I know. I am naive. I received no real insight into anything through these mirrors, in fact they just emphasised how uncomfortable I was, first of all to be in a dress, secondly to be in a white dress, which does nothing for my pale complexion, and thirdly to be in this decidedly creepy ritual, but I believed the hype and thought maybe I was just not faithful enough to see what everyone else appears to see. I did think that God should have known I don't suit white but I dismissed the thought as a triviality. I also thought that I found so much more truth in my grandad's small worn out mirror on his humble wall than in all these golden-encased floor to ceiling mirrors put together. But still the penny didn't drop. After a couple more visits, I knew enough to realise that most members go for three reasons, the cafeteria food which is slightly subsidised, to have a sleep during the boring repetitive instructional movie, or to look more righteous by tallying up temple session visits, because judging by the Sabbath day talks, the more you go to the temple, the more righteous you are. Another myth.

The Vegas temple, like all the others boasts of its natural light that streams through the large windows, projecting 'miniature rainbows on the walls', like a minor miracle occurs every time the sun shines. I have created the same effect in my kitchen with a cheap crystal. The obsession on light is, of course, symbolic. Dualism is alive and well, 'light' meaning you are spiritually enlightened and 'dark' meaning that you listen to Satan. Unfortunately, Isaiah 45:7 ('I form the light, and create darkness: I make peace, and create evil: I the Lord do all these things.') has been forgotten. What they fail to understand is that darkness is potential light. Maybe they would see more Divine Light if they reduced the electricity bill in their temples and meditated in the darkness where light is potentially present but stands silently waiting. Maybe, I am being harsh, after all Western culture teaches that light is a sacred landscape, Joseph Smith had his first encounter with God in a dark wooded grove where he wrestled with his doubts and it was in a shaft of sunlight that God appeared to tell him what to do and I too could have fallen into this way of thinking on this very trip when the sunlight hit my notebook in Santa Monica. The difference, however, is that for me monism brings everything together, darkness is storing light so it is all one. Robert Frost says it all in his succinct poem, 'Fire and Ice'.

Minutes turn into hours. My piano man is resting his aching ivory fingers and enjoying a tipple or two with what look like family members. The day has moved along without me noticing but Vegas understands my thinking. Her dark desert flowing gown embellished by millions of glowing sequins, attracts human moths by all things shiny. But to get to the light you have to go through the dark and they are both one. My day is coming to an end. My energy is waning and my hotel is calling.

I am aware this is my last day in Vegas and I make a point of enjoying the city at night from one of the many elevated pedestrian bridges connecting the hotels. She is as pretty as her famous showgirls and just as lively. She lights up with joy at night and parties until the moon outshines her beauty. It must look bizarre from the bird's eye view, a strip of neon in the pitch dark desert, draining the natural resources in a decadent peacock tail display of flirting.

I feel a weight has been lifted from my shoulders and I realise I am beginning to stop looking over my shoulder for judgemental associates and instead I am relaxing into the rhythm of this lovely place. If only 'those people' could see me now, they would think I have lost my mind, but ironically I believe I have found it. Vegas has given me a new rhetoric, a new belief in myself and the space to breathe. The old attic door has opened and I have stepped out of my closet prison into the sunlight. It has taken a while for my eyes to adjust but now that I can really see the neon illuminated speedway track that borders the Strip, outlining an array of flourescent flowered-shaped hotels, I realise the blinkers are being removed and my peripheral vision restored. People, like fireflies, dance a quickstep in choreographed beauty and suddenly I am washing my face in colour. No longer is this place a guilty pleasure. It is simply my pleasure.

I saw a wood pigeon walking up a steep sloping roof
She made it look easy
How?
Because she was not afraid of falling
She was expecting to be able to fly.

CHAPTER 18

It is always a mixture of emotions to leave the Vegas Strip. On one level it is very sad to have to get back to reality but on another level you know instinctively that you are only one more minute away from insanity if you stay. It is with such mixed feelings that it is time to say goodbye to my dancing fountains, all you can eat buffets, dazzling neon signs and the temptation of seeing Thunder Down Under. However, if one more porn calling card is thrust into my face, I might turn into arthritic ninja old lady, so I do comfort myself with the knowledge that I have so far acted with great dignity.

Vegas has been good and opened her arms to accept me as she always does, like an old lover or a prodigal child. Keeping true to her shallow honesty and deep truths, she welcomes me back with no judgement but sets me back on my feet and points me in the right direction. A different direction. The azure blue sky is breathtaking, the heat totally bearable in small doses (for someone like me who doesn't see too much sun) and Sin City is waving goodbye. With Ray Charles singing in my headphones, I am released.

I didn't see a magical sign, or indulge in a secret affair.
I didn't turn to drink or drugs or marry a millionaire.
But I opened up to face the pain
of the deceit 'those people' tried to maintain.
I allowed them to mould me into their clone
Ignorant of their undertones
I strived to be who they wanted me to be
Their captive in all of eternity.

If only I had known they were so inhumane
But
at last I have unlocked their binding
destructive chains.

Some would not thank you for the bus journey between LA and Vegas as the sun goes down and the light fades, but I love it. From the desert glimpses to daydreaming time and the passenger watching, it fascinates me, but it is a completely different experience to the daytime hustle and bustle of the previous bus ride. My fellow passengers have no words, they are Vegas-weary and ready for the comfort of their LA beds.

As soon as the light closes her eyes and the moon puts on his coat so the rhythm of the wheels sends me into a quiet moment of deep relaxation with whirling dreams and memories of Vegas. The reflective clouds of my mind play to the musical vibrations and rhythms of the engine's song. Too tired to contemplate my next move, I let myself fall into their arms.

The Best Western on Sunset attracts the bus to its final LA destination and as one of the last of the passengers to be released (the majority departing at Anaheim) I am glad to be staying here for a couple of days and not have a further taxi ride at this time of night. A very efficient doorman takes my bag and escorts me to the receptionist, who quickly sorts through the check-in process and I yawn my way up to my second floor room. This hotel is old school Hollywood, maybe in need of some tender loving care but I like the old fashioned air it greets me with and I half expect to see Clark Gable walk in with Marilyn Monroe on his arm.

An air conditioning unit sings an oratorio as I collapse on the bed and I remember wondering if trip advisor have complaints from light sleeping guests, but I love the melody as I close my eyes and dance into the dark. This is old Hollywood and she carries herself well.

The raven is watching through the window,
disguised by the night he silently waits and wonders.

Before I know it, the morning light entices me back to earth and the air conditioning welcomes me to announce it is time for breakfast. A quick shower and I am dressed ready for one of the last days left on my trip. A small but efficient lift takes me to the restaurant and I have a cheeky dance to the music enveloping me, what would 'those people' think? The breakfast area is smaller and cosier than other hotels but I don't mind that, it gives me some privacy to have a table to myself to consider what I have learned, whilst enjoying the most succulent blueberry muffin and a freshly squeezed neon orange juice. I have literally and emotionally come a long way from England via Vegas to LA, and quickly dismiss my theoretical pat on the back and replace it with a lecture on pride that I still hear in my head from 'those people'. After everything, they are still around my psyche but at least now I can recognise their voices much sooner and hopefully given time I will quieten their screaming. Somehow, my black and white world is accepting colour as my breakfast 'testifies'. I cringe at the use of that word, a remnant of the voice of 'those people', so quickly I catch my words and place them back in my mouth. Reviewing my choice of phrase, I decide to replace 'testify' with 'suggests' and decide not to dwell on it.

My time here is limited so I must make sure I have myself in place before I leave. Whether I am ready to get back to ordinary life or there is a sudden moment of intuition I don't know, but I decide to switch on my phone to check my emails for the first time in this whole trip.

There are a myriad of junk messages, nothing of any importance so I scroll my Facebook wall to see what I have missed in the world. There are a few cat videos which I pass over and the usual updates from people portraying their virtual perfect lives and then I see something that jumps out at me through the screen.

Letter to a CES Director by Jeremy Runnells.

In curiosity I opened the attached pdf file and my mind is officially blown wide open.

Jeremy, a member of good standing has been advised to write a letter to the Church Educational System, to express the questions he has after finding out the same information that I have on this journey. He is expecting to get some kind of answers to put his doubts at rest, or at least open up the opportunity for debate and discussion. I read his lengthy and detailed letter and discover he is concerned over the same topics that I have been torturing myself with. It is like he is reading my mind. This is a priesthood holder, from a direct pioneering ancestry, verbalising all my doubts in a very precise, yet non-judgemental way, in expectation of the promised response from leaders. Unbelievable. To think I am not alone in my quest after all this time is quite breath taking. Delving deeper I look anxiously for the official response, but he doesn't get one.

His fate now hangs in the balance as he awaits his 'court of love' which to the lay person is a very biased trial. He will be called to defend his name in front of local church leaders, which will end with at best, discreditation and worst excommunication (although it is fair to question which is the worst punishment in reality). His charge is that of apostasy, simply asking questions, the same 'apostate' label that is given to anyone who dares to enquire about the history of the Church, including no doubt, myself, although so far no one has actually said that word to my face. Still, it is enough to know that I am not alone, and that in itself gives me more validation that I could trust myself than I have received in many years. I contact him to offer my support and his quick response indicates that we share the same walk through doubt, disappointment and betrayal.

He is choosing to stay inside the organisation and face his potential excommunicators head on in a need to defend his request for answers. Only by escaping could I heal my own wounded unanswered questions. I hope he escapes too. Different human reactions but ultimately the same battle. His high profile posts on the internet have attracted a lot of media attention and it is of no surprise that church leaders are taking their time on this one. Keep your enemies close. The best part of this revelation is knowing that I am not alone anymore in this battle and also realising that I cannot change the unchangeable, I can only live my own truth and use my own moral compass. It will hurt less simply because I won't allow them to hurt me anymore. At least I am no longer alone. What an amazing feeling to know that the truth is seeping through the wireless wifi and into the world.

I was extremely delighted to learn later that Jeremy excommunicated the church from his life at his kangaroo court. After hitting the stone-wall suits head on, he took the power into his own hands and removed it from theirs.

Of course, Jeremy, like anyone else speaking out will face a character assassination, but I am grateful for his bravery. I had never heard the phrase 'lying for the Lord' until recently but this is the infallible 'get-out' clause for any of the top church authorities and I still don't understand it as we are taught to be honest at all times, but apparently if a leader is trapped in a corner cobweb of lies, 'lying for the Lord' in an attempt to protect the gospel is acceptable. There appears to be a lot of 'lying for the Lord'.

People ask why 'apostates' do not just leave the organisation and then leave it alone. Well this is no ordinary church. You cannot just stop going. If you do, you are judged, you are classed as inactive and will be the subject of many meetings to reactivate your sinful soul. You are assigned two home teachers, who are Priesthood holders, often a father and son who will visit you at home as part of their mission to get you back to church and the result will be reported back. You may also get visiting teachers, two female 'sisters' like my secret Santa couple, who too will report back on your situation. You are a statistic, a tick in some rigid box. The official line is that they are there for the support of your family, but the reality is that they are re-enforcing church policy, in your own home, subconsciously checking if you have the required church artwork on the walls, making sure there is no tea or coffee in your cupboards, and that your DVD collection has nothing rated fifteen or over. There is a strong likelihood that you will also get random visits from two missionaries, eighteen year olds who know little about this organisation, just the mission promoting brainwashing tidbits their brainwashed parents wanted them to hear. Regardless of your years of experience, you will be spoken to as if your church membership is non-existent and they will attempt to teach you from the beginning, platitudes you have heard a million times before. For the record despite those who now accuse me of it, I didn't lose my faith, but now it is very personal and does not have any reference to this cult, I also have no desire to impose it on others. If these teaching tactics don't work, you may get an invitation for a chat with the bishop or stake president, all of these leaders are lay men, untrained, unqualified, unpaid and uncompromising. They will passively threaten you.

My stake president told me that if I was determined to question then I must have committed a grave sin and basically laughed at me as he said that if I wasn't willing to admit to one then he would choose one to accuse me of at random. It made me sick to the core (hence the kidney failure shortly after). I saw the evil in his eyes. That is the moment I walked. That is the moment my life turned upside down and I realised if he was fake, then how much more of this stuff was made up. That is the day I showed immense dignity and self control by not punching him right between his smug eyes.

Oh yes, and people are still killing themselves because of the damage of this church. Suicide is currently increasing especially among the young LGBT community because they are simply not accepted. What can you do if you belong to a family that embraces this organisation and you are gay? Well, you will at best be tolerated and subtly asked to 'pray away the gay' and at worse ostracised from all friends, peers and family. It is a no-win situation. That is why it is hard not to speak out against it and just 'stop attending'. The current suicide rate amongst young LGBT church members in Utah is allegedly three times the rate it was just a few years ago with more names being silently added every week. But of course they tell you they love the sinner and hate the sin. Another glib phrase that I never understood, I love you but hate the way you sin by merely existing in your current form. Your actions, and your lifestyle abhor me, but I love you. Empty meaningless words. A delicate subject. A heap of church justifications. Dead children. I can't keep quiet. I was told on a daily basis to bear my witness of the truthfulness of this church. It is only fair that I now bear witness to the damage their lies cause.

In need of a distraction, I want to mark my freedom and start to express myself and Phil is just the guy. He is a renowned LA tattooist, 'those people' would say I rebelled too far but it is a small colourful California bear to honour my very basic animism and it is in a place that only I need to know, in memory of my experience and take note, it is extremely unlikely that you will ever see it. Having said that, my inner Vogue covergirl may yet materialise, so never say never, even us tomboys have our feminine moments, but safe to say you won't see me in a white dress.

Phil was recommended to me by a wonderful lady in

Book Soup, one of my favourite book stores. I came out with a copy of Emmet Fox, a free bookmark and a badge of Ralph Waldo Emerson to keep me on track and it turns out that Phil was the perfect tattooist for me. One of 'those people' once said to me that if anyone came to them for a job interview (which was unlikely because she lived off her rich corporate husband), she would instantly turn away anyone with tattoos or piercings. Now I objected to this and I told her so. I can appreciate it can be off putting for us oldies sometimes to accept life moves on but to cast someone aside just because of the way they look seems very unnecessary and very unfair. I thought about it and asked her why she wouldn't employ me. 'What do you mean?'

'Well, I have my ears pierced.'

'Oh, that's okay. That is acceptable.'

She was right. 'Those people' really do say that. So how about women getting their make-up tattooed on? Is that okay? Where is the line that you cross into the land of unacceptable? I am sure acupuncturists could argue against the wisdom of any piercing, but conveniently those women can wear their diamond earrings. It is all so ridiculous.

Phil is heavily tattooed. The inscription 'the pen is mightier than the sword' on his forearm confirms he is the right person and he is also a quite delightful artistic pierced punk. In our short time together, Phil taught me the beauty of unappreciated art in the professional tattoo world and Phil is a wonderful artist, there is no doubt about that. There is one thing that he excels in and that is colour. He is the master of all things colourful and yet, he dresses in black. All black. The reason that it works is because he knows who he is and he has enough colour in his world to pull off that look. So amid the reds and greens and yellows and blues in Phil's artistic world of tattoo art of snakes, flowers, birds, dragons, skulls, crosses and a myriad of other colourful designs, Phil taught me about black. A colour which threatens the canvas more than any other, irreversible, destructive and powerful, early representation of death and hell. The lifelong debate to decide whether or not black is a colour at all because it absorbs light and therefore is exempt from colour, puts it at a juxtaposition with the white canvas as white reflects all colours. As different as heaven or hell. I am sure there is a story to be told about Phil's (like Brando's) rebellious streak which is reflected by his choice of black. I am not an expert in chromatics, but I see it as his version of Shelley's melancholic romantic mystery. The war painted black warrior symbolises victory of the strong and brave and I can now dance in the cloak of black. The raven smiles.

Ornithological black vessel of potential light.

CHAPTER 19

Time to reflect. My notebook reads back my questions to me and I consider my new thoughts and answers.

Who was Joseph?

He was not the person they told me he was. They portrayed him as a spiritual giant, an inspirational prophet, a man of integrity, a representative of God on earth to be followed and obeyed. He was a fraud, a liar and he is now irrelevant to me. Joseph and 'those people' are no longer part of my life, or part of who I am.

What is true?

None of it was ever true. I am not who they told me to be. They remain happy in their delusional reality, but I don't have to buy into it anymore. I am evolving from cereal bar to blueberry muffin in the nicest way.

How do I find the elephant?

It can be a lifelong challenge to seek the elephant and some people don't even want to start looking, it is just too hard. It is seeking the fire in the soul, the fire that burns in your core. The fire that is your umbilical cord to Mother Earth. We ourselves are the truth we look for on our own pioneer trek. Seeking the elephant is the sign that you are still on your road to enlightenment, looking for happiness and contentment in the quest to bring you back to the person you set out to be from the very beginning. If you are still seeking the next challenge to prove your worth, the search to find your soulmate to make you complete, a bigger house, a promotion, a new car to make you feel successful, your quest is not complete.

The elephant is found in the dark silence of our minds, in the places that scare us and the spaces that most of us will do anything to avoid by filling that silence with any kind of noise. Only when you can look far enough within to unnerve you, will you realise that you were born the perfection you seek and only then can you let go and accept you are good enough without anything else.

How do I change my black and white world into colour?

Who knew the world out there has all the colours I needed, I just had to remove the blindfold. The world has never been more colourful to me.

It is my conclusion that humans are complicated souls and avoidance is often preferable. When everything you were taught turns out to be a lie, it changes your landscape forever, nothing is as it seems and suddenly I accept the realisation that learning to trust my innate self is a much more spiritual path than being brainwashed into an ideology based on manipulated events for personal corporate gain of immoral leaders.

Hollywood is a perfect reflection. TV home of all my

childhood memories, I wanted to make people laugh like Lucille Ball and be as beautifully delicate as Marilyn Monroe, but Hollywood, like Vegas, like life, is an illusion. Lucille Ball was chastised as a child for looking at herself in a mirror, no wonder she embraced adoration and she was not a natural red head. Marilyn tried to overcome her difficult childhood but her scars were so deep that unfortunately her death became as famous as her life and she was not a natural blonde.

Hollywood is full of broken people, all dying in front of your eyes, but most people don't see it. Hollywood is mentally ill, all the patients walk the same streets as their visitors and put on the show the world expects:

The prostitute who verbally attacks and chases you down the street is desperate for self-worth and knows nothing of her value.

The policeman whose hand shakes on the trigger of his gun, which he has drawn from his holster way too soon is scared of what you might do to him, but is particularly scared of himself and what he has become. Married to his job and addicted to adrenaline.

The homeless who are comforted by their cardboard beds medicate their way through the day in various ways, but these are the most authentic, they know they have already lost it all and are living in their own reality.

The Beverly Hills residents, who consist of pampered housewives, filling their empty hearts with beautiful things. Beautifying their botoxed bodies and filling their houses with shiny things to paint over their pain. Living on a treadmill of needing bigger, better and frightened to stop in case they fall off.

Their husbands who have sold their souls to Corporate America, talk in the language of business jargon as though they really believe it, staying at work too late to avoid their empty-hearted mansions and their trophy wives.

The trust fund children who know the value of nothing and the entitlement of everything, spiral out of control on a barrier free rollercoaster of disaster, that will eventually take their lives, and people think they are the lucky ones.

The tattooed people who visibly show their daily pain as an artwork on their outside, shouting out to express themselves, but people turn a deaf ear and cross the road to avoid, ostracise and judge, so their inked extremities which spell out 'hold me' go unseen and unread.

The alcoholics who gather together to comfort each other and people see their weakness and dismiss it as a lack of will power. We are all addicted to something.

The foolish addict is to be abhorred but the doctor who prescribes his wares to the Beverly Hills set is a saviour... or a murderer when things go wrong. He medicates himself to sleep to deal with the pressure.

The velvet red carpet heroes who hide their pain in prestigious parties and get shot a hundred times a day by the light bulbs of their predators and people say 'they had it all, why did it end so badly?'

Hollywood is cowering to the technology terrorist, where everything is made to sound perfect, look perfect and feel perfect, and is trying to keep pace with the gathering momentum to make sure they are not caught off guard by a wrong look or a wrong word forcing them to be left with a broken 'brand' and lose the spotlight.

Hollywood must appear as real as the traditional cosy Thomas Kinkade Christmas scene and people will clamour to recreate ultimate perfection in vain. But Hollywood is not alone. You live in the same movie. You play your own role in your amateur dramatic production, to 'wow' your audience, endeavouring to dodge your own paparazzi bullets until safely tucked up in bed at night, only to do it all again the next day. You maybe just don't do it on such a big scale, yours is not a full cast production but more of an independent film, maybe with sub titles, but we are all looking for the same empty pot of gold at the end of the rainbow.

You may say, 'how depressing', but if that is how you feel, you are still in scene one of your blockbuster movie, and there is a long way to go before the popcorn runs out. I am on a commercial break while I write this and I am looking reality in the face before the cameras start rolling again. Nothing is ever as it seems and once you accept that everything is possible. Sometimes gold is useless but an empty pot can hold water. Maybe just maybe one day we will heal each other. Until then at least Hollywood knows it is sick, but the tinsel on the hospital beds is very real.

CHAPTER 20

It is the penultimate day of my adventure when I discover online, to my despair, but also to my vindication, new official church essays, that have been leaked silently through a door of secretive duplicitousness on to the internet's maze of information. Here I have in front of my startled eyes the ultimate evidence, on the official church website all the information that would previously have been described to me as 'anti-mormon' propaganda to be avoided like a plague of locusts. Here it is, the same information that mormon historians previously have been excommunicated for suggesting it is truthful. Here it is. In murky grey, no colour in sight. There is a smell of desperation and damage limitation from leaders. Only now, after all this time, do they infer, in these various hastily produced documents of double speak, that they are now altering some of the major teachings that they imposed upon several generations. They tell us, that despite vehemently denying it, Joseph did actually have multiple wives, one as young as fourteen and many already married to other Priesthood holders. *Plural Marriage in Kirkland and Nauvoo* dances around the reasons for polygamy and infers that although Emma fought against Joseph's involvement, she eventually gave her consent to four such arrangements although also admits that she probably didn't know about all of the rest of her devoted husband's dalliances. You have to look at the small print at the end of the document to see that the church now estimates Joseph was in such relations with between thirty and forty women. Emma knew about four of them, remember, according to them. I still have my doubts about how much Emma knew. Liars.

The *Book of Mormon Translation* essay tells us that Joseph was indeed a treasure seeker and did have a seer stone that helped him translate the Book of Mormon. It also states that he did put it in his hat into which he pressed his face for inspiration (just as depicted on an episode of South Park that at the time many members including myself laughed at as being ridiculous). The church official art has never shown Joseph using this method, instead he is usually sitting at a table by candlelight studying the scriptures, with no hat or stone in sight. How many Sunday School lessons have I not only attended, but also taught where these incorrect images are displayed? I am left with a caricature version of a man pulling a rabbit out of a hat. If it wasn't so tragic, it would be funny.

The *First Vision Accounts* reports, for the first time ever to my knowledge, that there are several versions of the 'first' vision in which Joseph was visited by God with instructions for organising the church and these versions contradict each other in many details, which I find completely mind-boggling. The foundation of the church is built on this vision and yet even that is now altered, tarnished, rewritten. It was the first of several extremely unreliable visions, not the one unique experience that was taught to us daily. Everything I believed is not only broken, but thrown against the wall and as the damaged words slide down the stonework they are stomped on by a hobnailed boot.

In the essay, *Race and the Priesthood*, all the teachings about the curse of black skin are forgotten and in their words 'disavowed' (although the scriptures remain unchanged so probably the meanings of the words are now no longer literal but symbolic, which is the easiest get out clause). In an attempt to quieten the racist teachings of the past, they literally wash their hands of ever admitting doing it in the first place. If one word sums up this organisation, it is 'disavow', they own no responsibility for anything.

Book of Mormon and DNA Studies explains how they now call the Book of Mormon more spiritual than historical, presumably because DNA evidence is not working out for them. It was always taught as being actual history, complete with maps and historic timelines, which can now be forgotten and/or waived away also as being symbolic like any other awkward uncomfortable truth.

The most disturbing thing is that it appears few members are even aware of these essays and even fewer missionaries, but this is all part of the marketing plan to deal with difficult people like me. Remember, if they can ease these new truths in, then once my generation and possibly some of the next are history, the new generations will not know half of the things we were taught and there will be a whole new set of convenient truths. The saddest

142

part is that some members, even when made aware of the essays, will rationalise the information and convince themselves that they knew these things all along and so the work moves on.

Although I never expected the production of such essays, they confirm to me a sense of official back-peddling guilt that only further serves to disgust me, although by now I am numb to it at the same time. Nothing surprises me anymore as I now know the depths of the deception. My only consolation is that I am glad to know for sure I was lied to, because it makes it easier to know that all my doubts and confusion have been for a reason. Things didn't add up and I was questioning the very subjects they had no answers for. No wonder I pissed them off. It doesn't matter to me now. These are meaningless colourless platitudes that have no purpose. I cannot express adequately enough how I gain no pleasure from finally having confirmation of my doubts. There is no reward to feeling deceived, duped and fooled but at least I know I am not going mad after all and maybe now I can trust myself. It is awkwardly cleansing. The voice of 'those people' has disappeared in the mist of mayhem they have created with their lies and my voice is emerging. Vindication at last, but I still want to weep for those currently being deceived, especially those who are living in a lie because the alternative is unacceptable in heaven. My eyes are open, the birds are singing colour and the world is opening her arms in a welcoming embrace.

A brief visit to the Hollywood and Highland centre gives me the chance to compose my thoughts and allows me back into the real world.

It is an eventful trip which leads me through a very talented mariachi band, a convention of young people at a severed head convention (although it might be some sort of beauty or hairdressing event as the heads were not entirely convincing) and most enjoyably, I am accosted by a lovely young man, which hasn't happened for a very long time. He seems to recognise that I am admiring his uniquely styled t-shirt and with no actual recordable conversation, he removes his headphones and dances over towards me sharing his rap music and his moves. My silent companion allows me to dance with him briefly and I have never felt so alive. He has no idea what that small gesture means to me but I hope the universe rewards him.

I treat myself to some new shoes, a Christmas ornament which is in no way religious, a very tasty smoothie and engage in some people watching. The water display that jumps up to surprise and delight all ages is in top form. Children run through the strategically-placed fountains and avoid getting too wet, but they don't care. Adults vary. Some are horrified by the idea of getting wet and walk around it, some fling off their shoes and dance like their child inside, others are wary but by being cautious they allow the water to find them and end up getting soaked, much to the amusement of their friends. Some people are ready to embrace a fountain of fun and some are uncomfortable with the chance to play. We are back to the elephant.

My time here is now limited. The reality of home is calling. It is another goodbye, but I am not the same person who arrived here and once more my trusted landscape has healed my soul, so although I leave with reluctance, I can embrace the happiness that Nature's parents have once more reminded me of. Tawdry Vegas and the horrors of Hollywood have taught me more than the faux paradisiacal, ultra cleanliness, sinless views of 'those people'. The landscape knows our secrets.

**The poetry of pavements and the symmetry of
sidewalks
hold the stories from the soles of their pedestrian feet.
Everyday, unnoticed urban dialogues
of ramblers, travellers and the man in the street.**

Be mindful where you plant your feet.

CHAPTER 21

Today I prepare myself for the necessity of the flight back home. Space in my suitcase is valuable and there is a book I don't need to travel with anymore. What can I do with it? I don't want to leave it for someone else. That would be like leaving the rest of your drugs for a friend to try while you go to rehab. I can't burn it... taboo. I can't rip it up, that just seems wrong. Maybe I am overthinking it. I could throw it in the bin, maybe then it will return to the soil it came from and make some valuable compost, but perhaps it will contaminate the soil. Anyway, I don't need the book anymore. I will think of something.

I am sending my official resignation by email to the Church headquarters today, although I left a long time ago. It is essential to resign so that they no longer control what I do. I do not want to be part of their creative statistical analysis that discusses how fast they are growing when they do not admit to how fast they are losing members. I guess the fact that I feel the need to 'resign' from a church should tell me something. I do not expect an immediate reply. Experience tells me that I will be ignored, then forced to wait and constantly chase them up, especially as their official instructions tell the leaders, between the lines, to 'sit on' any such requests to delay proceedings. However, I will get a written acknowledgement because

I will no longer be invisible. This church has been more disabling than any illness and it is time to peel off the labels they gave me. You cannot be a successful victim but you can be a successful survivor. My physical scars no longer trespass on my landscape, instead my golden repairs glimmer in the Californian sunlight. Nothing has physically changed but everything has improved, that is the dichotomy.

My time in this wonderful place is at an end and my reality calls. The landscape has not let me down, Mother Earth has embraced me with love and guidance, wiped away my tears and set me back on my feet to help ground me. I am forever grateful.

The ride to the airport is as enjoyable as all goodbyes and LAX is as busy as ever, but it is no use fighting the inevitable, I must get back to my everyday life. As I board the plane, preparing for my return into the supporting arms of Father Sky, I am transforming into the person I always was, no longer hiding from myself or anyone else. Now, I still might not be one of those Vogue women but I can become one if I want to. The truth is that I don't really care if I choose not to carry off the elegant blanket over my head look. There are no more limitations that I place on myself, my silent companion and I will work together to embrace the rest of the time we have together.

I feel different. They no longer have a hold on me. I am my authentic self for the first time since that small girl gazed at her own hopeful reflection. The family fears are the fallen petals of a bouquet of roses presented to me as a gift to learn from and then release back to the earth. This gesture has repaired the broken branches of my family tree and their voices combine with mine, in support of all those external forces that imposed the fear that wounded us. My opportunity to speak for those wounded by war propaganda, whose dying breath fell against the stench of the trenches. For those who couldn't put right the wrongs of war, for the boys who lost who they were, to become soldiers for a day, crying into the dead of night for a mothers' love. For those who trusted and lost loved ones and no one heard their silent screams. I fell into the arms of 'those people' through my inherited vulnerability and fears but I jumped out of their clutches with the courageous integrity given to me graciously by previous generations and all without the aid of a parachute. Lifted on the wings of Father Sky, I floated safely down to my own truth, but I endured the storm first. I have found my stifled voice. I am no longer invisible.

At last they will hear my voice screaming from the mountain top, in glorious multicolour.

As the plane soars to greater heights, it is with a wry smile that I travel back home with the knowledge that Richie the Barber, the resident Hollywood clown, with his miniature black bowler hat, his bright yellow shirt and red and white polka dot waistcoat, has some rather unusual addition to his sparkling confetti as he delights the unexpected passengers today. He is spreading the joy, spreading the blue, pink, red, yellow, purple, orange, green, black and white, gold and silver and the myriad of colours in-between. He is spreading the word. It is all in a good cause. May the colours touch every aspect of your life.

May it be beautiful
before me.
May it be beautiful
behind me.
May it be beautiful
All around me.
In beauty
It is finished;
In beauty
It is finished.

Traditional Dinah (Navajo chant)